NO
ADMITTANCE
eland's
Pale

THE American Brewery

FROM COLONIAL EVOLUTION TO MICROBREW REVOLUTION

Bill Yenne

MBI

First published in 2003 by MBI Publishing Company,Galtier Plaza, Suite 200, 380 Jackson Street, St. Paul, MN 55101-3885 USA

On the front cover: Founded by Mark Stutrud, the Summit Brewing Company began operations in 1986 and tripled its capacity in 1993 through the lease of a building behind the original St. Paul brewery. By the turn of the century, annual output had topped 45,000 barrels, and in 2002 Summit became the largest brewery in Minnesota. *Summit Brewing via Chuck Anderson, ABZ Group*

On the back cover: The F. & M. Schaefer Brewing Company as it appeared on a warm summer day in July 1948. *Library of Congress via author's collection*

On the endpapers: This group photo, circa 1890, features the staff of John Wieland's Brewery in San Francisco. Most of the employees who were included in the photo were brewery wagon drivers. The labels on the kegs touted the brewery's in-house bottling line. *San Francisco History Center via author's collection*

On the title page: Nineteenth-century craftsmanship is evident in this gleaming copper brew kettle on the floor of the Tivoli-Union Brewery. Most of the equipment was installed at the time of construction. *Library of Congress via author's collection*

On the table of contents page: You can almost feel the chill on the glass in this beautifully airbrushed ad art that Ballantine used around 1950. *Author's collection*

Library of Congress Cataloging-in-Publication

Yenne, Bille, 1949-
The American brewery / by Bill Yenne
p. cm.
ISBN 0-7603-1470-5 (alk. paper)
1. Beer--History. 2. Brewing industry--United States--History. I. Title.

TP573.U6Y46 2003
338.4'766342'0973--dc21

Edited by Dennis Pernu

Designed by Tom Heffron

Printed in Hong Kong

CONTENTS

America's
Largest Selling Ale
BALLANTINE'S
295 MADISON AVENUE
PURITY BODY FLAVOR
XXX
BREWED & BOTTLED BY
P. BALLANTINE & SONS
NEWARK
NEW JERSEY
ALE
CONTENTS 12 FLUID OZ
INTERNAL REVENUE

ACKNOWLEDGMENTS

In the course of writing about beer and brewing for nearly two decades, I am indebted to many people in the industry who have shared their time and resources, especially those who supplied the photographs that were used in this book. Fritz Maytag and Mark Carpenter at Anchor Brewing come to mind; they were among the first to offer encouragement, and they remain supportive two decades later. Others who have been more than helpful, both on earlier projects and on this work, include Jeff Waalkes of Miller Brewing, as well as Dan Gordon and Dana Kemberling of Gordon Biersch. People such as Jack Joyce at Rogue, Tom Allen of North Coast Brewing, and Don Shook of Adolph Coors have provided valuable material through the years. I have learned a great deal about the beer more ancient than that of George Washington from Alan Eames, the eminent beer archeologist. Charles Finkel, an internationally recognized beer expert and importer, has been a good friend and a tireless champion of beer as part of the currency of civilized society. Allan Paul of San Francisco Brewing deserves a special nod of thanks for his extraordinary beer and his continuous great generosity over many years. Finally, thanks to Dennis Pernu of MBI Publishing Company, who has been the most enthusiastic and involved editor I have ever worked with on a project related to beer and brewing.

Cheers!

BREWING AND CIVILIZATION

Brewing has been part of civilized society since the dawn of history. Knowing that leaves one to wonder how beer has changed and evolved in that time. In 1989, Professor Solomon Katz of the University of Pennsylvania and Fritz Maytag and the Anchor Brewing Company in San Francisco set out to answer that question by attempting, in Maytag's words, to "duplicate mankind's earliest professionally brewed beer."

First presented at the Microbrewery Conference in September 1989 and available commercially for a few months thereafter, the beer was named "Ninkasi," after the Sumerian goddess of brewing. The beer itself was a re-creation of a Sumerian beer that had been brewed around 2,800 B.C. Katz located the ancient recipe, and Maytag devoted the resources of a modern state-of-the-art brewery to actually brew a beer based on a formula that hadn't been used in centuries. The result was an unhopped, honey-sweet beer unlike anything familiar to modern palates.

In this project, Katz and Maytag completed a circle, bringing the revitalized American craft-brewing industry into touch with the state of the brewer's art at the beginning of civilization.

INTRODUCTION

The art and science of brewing beer have been a part of civilization for centuries. Some scholars have even gone so far as to posit brewing as a cornerstone of civilization. Professor Solomon Katz, an archeologist at the University of Pennsylvania, advanced the theory that humankind first domesticated grain not to bake bread but to brew beer!

Beer was brewed at least as early as 2,800 B.C., and it was very much part of life throughout the ancient world. It tempered the lives and loves of the Sumerians, the Egyptians, and perhaps even Moses himself. The ancient Egyptians believed that their goddess Hathor had invented beer. Records show that during Egypt's Middle Kingdom (about 1,800 B.C.), 130 jars of beer were delivered daily to the royal court. One day it was recorded that the queen herself received five jars. Oh, to have been a fly on the wall during *that* splendid afternoon on the shores of the Nile!

The art and science of brewing beer have been a part of American civilization since before that group of late-eighteenth-century patriots first conceived the notion of the United States. As we shall see in the opening chapter of this work, beer came to North America on the *Mayflower*, although the indigenous people of the continent were already brewing beer. Later, men such as George Washington and Thomas Jefferson were not only brewers themselves, they were both promoters of a quality beer's value to society.

The art and science of brewing beer have also paralleled the evolution of the United States. During the nineteenth century, as the nation grew expansive and as it embraced the Industrial Revolution, the American brewing industry followed—on both counts. As that century began, breweries, like other factories, were the small shops of craftsmen. Their beer was produced by hand, in small quantities, in the manner of craftsmen. As the nineteenth century closed, breweries were massive, imposing, redbrick structures, each of which employed hundreds and produced thousands of barrels of beer.

In their 1933 work, *Brewing Industry and Brewing Science in America*, John Arnold and Frank Penman summarized this evolution, writing "It is doubtful if all history can present another chapter as curious as that of the American brewing industry, how, after going along for centuries in a quiet, unassuming way, largely as a household occupation, it took a spurt and within half a century grew to be one of the biggest industries of the country."

By the early twentieth century, America's great industrial base was expanding and maturing into a global powerhouse that was second to none. Yet the brewing industry was faced with a situation unique among American industries. At its peak, it was suddenly, in the words of Arnold and Penman, "cut off and destroyed by Prohibition," only to be just as suddenly "resurrected by popular demand and hailed with general acclaim." American brewing had survived and flourished.

A generation later, when the American brewing industry threatened itself by growing stale and bland, the brewers again rallied to save a tradition. With the Microbrewery Revolution of the 1980s, the industry came full circle. American brewing was reinvented in the small shops of the craftsman. Once again, American brewing survives and flourishes.

Chapter 1 Beer Arrives in America 1607–1776

The notion of "coming over on the *Mayflower*" used to describe an existence in North America since the continent's earliest days of European colonization. Beer did, indeed, come over on the *Mayflower*. When the crew began to run short of supplies, they dropped the pilgrims at Plymouth, instead of at the mouth of the Hudson River as planned, and headed for home, keeping the beer that remained. According to Edward Winslow, author of *Mourt's Relation: A Journal of the Pilgrims at Plymouth, 1622,* "We could not now take time for further search or consideration, our victuals being much spent, especially our beer."

If the history of American breweries were a Hollywood movie, this true story would make a wonderful opening scene, but this beer was not the *first* beer quaffed within sight of American shores. The native peoples of both North and South America had been brewing beer for centuries. In 1778, Captain James Cook observed that the natives of Vancouver Island, in what is now British Columbia, enjoyed spruce beer. However, little is known about these pre-Columbian brewing traditions because the first Europeans to have contact with most native people had little interest in preserving information about their traditions.

In what is now the United States, the plateaus and canyons of the Southwest may have been home to some of the earliest American breweries. As we know from the early Spanish explorers, many indigenous people in Mexico and the Southwest brewed a beer that the Spanish called *tiswin* or *tesguino.* This beer was produced until the latter part of the nineteenth century. While Europeans—then and now—use barley as the fermentable starch, the Native Americans used corn. For them, corn was a dual-purpose cereal grain.

Opposite: *New Amsterdam was a major brewing center early in the seventeenth-century American colonies. In this old engraving of the city's commercial district, one can imagine that brewing is taking place in at least one of these buildings.* Author's collection

Above: *Beer came to America in 1620 on the* Mayflower, *but the crew retained it aboard ship after they dropped the pilgrims off at Plymouth Rock. If they had not been running short of beer, the crew would have taken their passengers to the Hudson River Valley.* Author's collection

Once stockpiled in a corn crib, it could either be eaten or used for beer making. This was a common paradigm in the ancient world. In ancient Sumeria, barley was baked into *bappir* loaves that could be warehoused for food or for use in brewing. The Sumerians flavored their beer with honey, while Europeans flavored and preserved their beer with a bittering agent such as hops. Coincidentally, the Pueblo people of the Southwest also bittered—rather than sweetened—their beer. Instead of hops, Pueblos used juniper.

Europeans had little or no use for the pre-Columbian breweries in North America, and these disappeared before any ethnographer could seriously study them. The same is true of the earliest European breweries in the New World, which probably existed in Mexico in the sixteenth century.

However, within a few months of establishment in 1607, beer was imported into the London Company's Jamestown Colony in Virginia. Records show that the company was planning for brewers to be sent to the colony in 1609. Farther north, in Plymouth Colony, it was recorded that the pilgrims who had been left without beer when the *Mayflower* turned home craved it, but did not brew it. Even the straight-laced Puritans, who established the nearby Massachusetts Bay Colony a few years later, did not describe beer as sinful, but as essential. The Puritan minister Richard Mather wrote in 1635 of "wholesome beere."

After the arrival of beer, breweries were soon to follow. Nobody is sure of the date or location of the first European brewery in what is now the United States, but the historical record shows that several were in operation around Massachusetts Bay and in Virginia by the 1630s. One of the earliest Massachusetts brewers mentioned by name was Robert Sedgewick, who was active in Charlestown by this time.

In order to regulate public drunkenness, Massachusetts Bay Colony originally did not permit taverns to brew their own beer, but this law was relaxed in 1639. Although it is unknown exactly who opened it or specifically where it was located, the first brewpub in Boston began operation in 1639. Today, colleges and universities often exist in proximity to brewpubs. America's first institution of higher learning, Harvard College (now Harvard University) in Cambridge, was founded in 1636. Within a few years, Harvard probably had a brewpub nearby, but it is most remarkable for having its own on-campus brewery by at least 1674, and possibly as early as 1667. Harvard would continue to make beer routinely available to its students for more than a century, but the practice eventually faded. In 1814, the last of three Harvard brewhouses was burned down by underclassmen.

Despite these recorded events, the first American brewpub was not in Boston, nor was the true center of brewing in North America in the English colonies. The Netherlands West India Company established its first two North American colonies in 1623, with the linchpin settlement at

Left: *Captain John Carver and Massasoit formalize the treaty between Plymouth Colony and the Wampanoag people. The legendary—and possibly apocryphal—early Thanksgiving celebrations brought these two groups together peacefully. If such a feast did take place, beer would have certainly been on the table.* Author's collection

Above: *Typical of eighteenth-century Philadelphia establishments where beer was served and probably brewed was the colorfully named Man Full o' Trouble Tavern. Built in 1759, it had fallen into disrepair when this moody photo was taken in 1961, but it was subsequently restored. Today, it is the only surviving pre-Revolutionary tavern in Philadelphia.* Library of Congress via author's collection

New Amsterdam on Manhattan Island coming several years later. The West India Company built the first commercial brewery in New Amsterdam in 1632 on what came to be known as *Brouwerstraat* (Brewer's Street, now Stone Street). The appellation "Manhattan beer" soon became synonymous with beer of high quality.

By the end of the decade, breweries proliferated throughout New Amsterdam and at other sites along the Hudson River to the north, as well as throughout the colony of New Netherlands.

The Bayard brothers—Balthazar, Nicholas, and Peiter—who were nephews of Peter Stuyvesant, the governor of New Netherlands, operated one of the earliest New Amsterdam breweries. Just north of present-day Wall Street, The Red Lion Brewery brewed what was probably America's first name-brand beer. Founded in 1660 by Isaac de Forest, it survived until 1675, when it was destroyed by fire.

Above: *The Three Tun Tavern at Mount Holly, New Jersey, was a combination brewpub and inn built by Samuel Briant before 1737. The name clearly confirms that brewing beer was a key activity here. Indeed, if three lauter tuns were present, the quantity of beer produced there would have been substantial. When this photograph was taken in March 1937, the establishment had become the Mill Street Hotel. As the sign suggests, patrons were still being served "draught" beer.* Library of Congress via author's collection

Right: *The old Piscataway Tavern, a.k.a. Claggetts' Tavern, on Piscataway Road in Prince George's County, Maryland, was typical of an eighteenth-century roadhouse where a traveler might enjoy a fresh pint and a plate of roast beef, and then possibly pass the night. When photographed in April 1936, it was little changed from its heyday.* Library of Congress via author's collection

Little is known of this old roadside tavern near Queen Anne in Talbot County, Maryland, which was on the verge of collapse when photographed in April 1936. Note the third chimney, which suggests that a kitchen was once kept busy not only cooking, but also boiling mash. Library of Congress via author's collection

Below: *The Dutch colonists of seventeenth-century New Amsterdam, like their contemporaries in the English colonies of Massachusetts and elsewhere, enjoyed drinking their beer from pewter mugs such as the one pictured here.* Author's collection

One of the practical considerations that obviously governed the evolution of brewing in America was the availability of ingredients. Neither barley nor commercially grown hops were widely available initially, so the early seventeenth-century brewers made do with what they had.

The Dutch in North America are believed to have made use of indigenous wild hops before the English, who used spruce as a bittering agent in place of hops. The English, like the Native Americans of the Southwest, used corn instead of barley as a fermentable starch. In this sense, the early beer produced by the Massachusetts brewers had more in common with the tesguino of the Pueblos than it did with London ale. By the end of the seventeenth century, however, barley was well established as one of New England's key cash crops.

Strategically located between the English colonies in Virginia and Massachusetts, New Amsterdam quickly became one of the key trading cities in North America. In 1664, it also became English. The Duke of York (who was later dubbed King James II) intimidated Peter Stuyvesant into surrendering New Netherlands without a shot being fired, and New Amsterdam was promptly renamed in honor of the Duke. The political changes seem not to have disturbed the brewing activities in the slightest, and the Dutch brewers did not miss a beat, as their city became New York. Indeed, the English soon supported the brewing industry by levying taxes on wine and rum, while exempting beer and cider that had been produced in the colonies.

By the time New Amsterdam became New York, there were small breweries cropping up throughout English-speaking North America, from Rhode Island to Georgia. William Penn, the founder of Pennsylvania, like many of his fellow Quakers, was fond of beer and featured it prominently in his famous 1683 treaty with the Indians. It was at about this time when Penn built a 700-square-foot brewery on his own estate near Bristol. Although his house soon burned down, the Penn brewery survived until 1864, nearly two centuries later.

In 1683, the same year that Penn built his brewhouse, William Frampton, a Quaker from New York started the first commercial brewery in Philadelphia. It was located on Front Street near Dock Street in Pennsylvania's chief port and largest city. It would take eight decades, but the brewer's art finally crossed the Alleghenies in 1765, when His Majesty's army built the first brewery of the West at Fort Pitt, which is today's Pittsburgh.

Philadelphia soon emerged second only to New York as an American brewing center. Among the more important brewers, the Emlens were a prosperous Quaker merchant family who supplied beer throughout the city for at least three generations. Located on Fifth Street, the Emlen Brewery also provided sustenance for ships that were fitted out in Philadelphia's harbor.

Small neighborhood breweries and brewpubs remained important in Philadelphia as well. One such place where beer was served—and probably brewed—was the colorfully named Man Full o' Trouble Tavern. Built in 1759, it was operated by Michael Sisk until 1773, when James Alexander took over to guide it through the Revolutionary period. Martha Smallwood became the site's first woman publican in 1796. The establishment was later known as Stafford's Tavern, the Cove Cornice House, and Naylor's Hotel. Today, it is the only surviving pre-Revolutionary tavern in Philadelphia.

Beyond the major brewing centers in New York, Philadelphia, and Boston, taverns also continued to routinely brew their own beer throughout the eighteenth century. Among the more interesting establishments was the Three Tun Tavern at Mount Holly, New Jersey. Built by Samuel Briant before 1737, its name clearly confirms that brewing beer was an important activity. Indeed, if three lauter tuns—the vessels in which barley husks are separated from the wort—were present, the quantity of beer being produced would have been substantial.

Through the years, the tavern and its inn had numerous famous patrons. During the Revolutionary War, Lord Cornwallis occupied rooms at the Three Tun. The name was changed to the Square & Compass early in the nineteenth century, and in 1805 it became a meeting place of the Masonic order. In 1825, it was renamed as the Sign of General Jackson after Andrew Jackson. During Prohibition, the establishment became the Mill Street Hotel.

Early in the eighteenth century, brewing spread beyond the Northeast and Virginia. In Baltimore, the first major brewery seems to have been started in 1748 by Elias Daniel Barnitz and his brother John. While John dropped out after a year, Elias remained involved with the company for more than three decades. In the South, Major William Horton constructed a brewery at Jekyll Island, Georgia, in 1738, and in 1774 the Single brothers established a brewery in Salem, North Carolina. By this time, other breweries were noted along the Mississippi River and well beyond the colonies that would form the original thirteen states. In 1765, a brewery was established at the French colonial settlement of Kaskaskia in what is now Illinois.

Above: *New Amsterdam Governor Wouter van Twiller and his colleagues enjoy fresh beer—direct from the keg—while observing the harbor. This old illustration also shows a variety of drinking vessels, including several types of glassware.* Author's collection

William Penn, founder of Pennsylvania, enthusiastically supported and encouraged brewing in his colony. He also constructed his own brewhouse in Bristol. The building would survive for two centuries. Author's collection

HOWARD & FULLER'S
ALE & PORTER BREWERY.
BRIDGE ST.
OFFICE
DELIVERY FLOOR
MAIN CARTWAY

They were the founding fathers of both America and American brewing. George Washington brewed beer, as did fellow Virginia aristocrat Thomas Jefferson.

Of course, a great deal is made of the fact that the famous revolutionary, Samuel Adams of Boston, also brewed beer. However, he is believed to have been a maltster—one who prepared barley kernels for the brewing process—rather than a brewer. Nevertheless, Adams was an integral part of the eighteenth-century American brewing industry, just as he was simultaneously an integral part of the radical wing of the movement to liberate the colonies from mother England.

Indeed, the colonial brewing industry was an integral part of the movement toward independence. In the wake of the French & Indian War, the British government attempted to raise money for colonial defense through a series of draconian taxes on the colonists. First came the short-lived Stamp Act, passed in 1765 and repealed a year later. Next came the more wide-ranging Townshend Acts passed by the English Parliament in 1767. These acts called for taxation that cut deeply into the lives and pocketbooks of colonists with taxes on everything from beer to tea.

Samuel Adams, who had been one of the leading protesters against these taxes, was also a leader of the group of colonists who disguised themselves as Native Americans and boarded British tea ships in Boston harbor on the night of December 16, 1773. They might just as well have been beer ships, although most beer—while still subject to British taxation—was brewed locally.

Opposite: *Junius Fuller began his English-style ale and porter brewery at Bridge and Plymouth in Brooklyn, New York, in 1835. William Howard would join the firm in 1854, and the company would continue to operate until 1914. Howard & Fuller's establishment was a typical example of breweries with roots that preceded the Lager Revolution.* Author's collection

George Washington was a gentleman farmer and home brewer who made his home at Mount Vernon in Virginia. He also served as commander of the Continental Army during the American Revolution and, of course, later as President of the United States. His love for beer, especially the Philadelphia porter of Robert Hare, is well documented. Library of Congress via author's collection

In the eighteenth century, locally brewed beer was just that—local. In colonial times, large commercial breweries as we know them did not yet exist. The brewing industry comprised brewers whose radius of distribution was analogous to that of the local bakery. A village brewer would usually brew for the village, or, in the case of a city, for the narrow confines of the neighborhood or a portion of the city. A maltster, on the other hand, might supply malt for a number of brewers over a wider radius.

As with many industries, brewing and malting were family businesses. For example, Samuel Adams' great-grandfather, Joseph Adams, is recorded to have been a 1690s maltster in Braintree, Massachusetts. His descendants followed in the business.

In New York City, the Rutgers family—the Dutch ancestors of Colonel Henry Rutgers, who in 1825 endowed the university of the same name—emerged as one of the city's most important brewers. The Rutgers Brewery was located on Stone Street, which had been known as *Brouwerstraat* (Brewer's Street) when the Dutch owned Manhattan. One of many breweries in the city, the Rutgers establishment would be a fixture in lower Manhattan through much of the eighteenth century until destroyed by fire in 1783.

As noted earlier, Philadelphia became one of the most important brewing centers in colonial America, and the Emlen family was an important brewing dynasty in the city. It is little wonder that in 1777, before moving into winter quarters at nearby Valley Forge, George Washington made his headquarters at the home of George Emlen III. One can imagine the general and his gracious host quaffing mugs of fresh beer.

Washington was an aficionado of Philadelphia beer. It is well known that he patronized a Philadelphia brewer named Benjamin Morris, and that he favored the porter brewed by Robert Hare, also of Philadelphia. An expatriate Englishman, Hare is believed to have been the first American brewer to produce this smooth, dark style of beer that originated in 1722 with London brewer Ralph Harwood. In London, Harwood's creamy invention had quickly become popular with tradesmen—especially porters.

(48)

One half pint of Rice, or one pint of Indian meal pr Man, pr Week.
One quart of Spruce Beer pr man, pr diem, or 9 Gallons of molasses pr Company of 100 Men.
Three pounds of Candles to 100 Men pr Week, for Guards &c.
Twenty-four pounds of soft, or eight pounds of hard Soap for 100 Men per week.
One Ration of Salt, one ditto fresh, and two ditto Bread, to be delivered Monday morning; Wednesday morning the same.
Friday morning the same, and one ditto salt Fish.
All weekly allowances delivered Wednesday morning, where the number of Regiments are too many to serve the whole the same day, then the Number to be divided equally, and one part served Monday Morning, the other part Tuesday Morning, and so through the week.

Head Quarters, Cambridge, August 9th 1775.
Parole Rochester. Countersign. Plymouth.
The Commanding Officer of each Regiment, or Corps, is to send a Return at Orderly time, to morrow to the Adjutant General, of the number of Tents or boards, which are wanted to cover the men, that they may be provided as soon as possible. They are also to give in the Names of such of their men, who neither have received Blankets, or who lost them in the engagement, on Bunkers-hill.
As there are several Vacancies in the different Regiments,

Right: *On August 8, 1775, General George Washington ordered that rationed provisions allowed by the Continental Congress for each soldier should include "One quart of Spruce Beer per man, per diem, or 9 Gallons of molasses."* Library of Congress via author's collection

(147)

Dollars, to pay their men for their Blankets, an exact account of the distribution of this money is to be kept, and render'd when call-ted for, particularizing the mens names, the Companies they belong to, and the towns they come from.

The Captains of the Militia Companies are again called upon to make out exact Return Rolls of their men specify-ing the towns they come from, and the Regiment they are joined to.

The General expects from the Officers, and Soldiers, a strict obedience to the general standing Orders, forbidding ramb-ling from Camp without leave, and hopes every person will exert himself in his particular station, to preserve Order, and that alert-ness so necessary in an Army within Cannon Shot of their enemy.

Head Quarters, Cambridge, Decr 24th 1775

Parole Alfred. Countersign Hopkins

By order of his Excellency General Washington, a Board of General Officers sat yesterday in Cambridge, and unanimously recommended the following Rations to be delivered in the manner hereby directed. — Viz.

Corn'd Beef and Pork, four days in a week.
Salt Fish one day, and fresh Beef two days.
As Milk cannot be procured during the Winter Season, the Men are to have one pound and a half of Beef or eigh-teen Ounces of Pork pr day.
Half pint of Rice, or a pint of Indian Meal pr week —

one

(148)

One Quart of Spruce Beer pr day, or nine Gallons of Molasses to one hundred Men pr week.
Six pounds of Candles to one hundred Men pr week for guards.
Six Ounces of Butter, or nine Ounces of Hogs Lard pr week.
Three pints of Pease, or Beans pr Man pr week, or Vegetables equivalent, allowing Six Shillings pr Bushel for Beans, or Pease — two and eight pence pr Bushel for Onions — One and four pence pr Bushel for Potatoes and Turnips.
One pound of Flour pr man each day — Hard Bread to be dealt out one day in a week, in lieu of Flour.

The above allowance is ordered to be issued by the Commissary General to all the Troops of the United Colonies, serving in this department until the Honble the Continental Congress, or the Commander in Chief thinks proper to alter it.

Capt. Wentworth Stewart of Col Phinny's Regt tried at a General Court Martial whereof Col Bricket was president for "disobedience of Orders, and gross abuse to Lieut Col March of the said Regiment." The Court are unanimously of opinion that Capt Stewart is guilty of repeated abuse to Lieut Col March, and there-fore adjudge that he ask pardon of Col March, before all the Of-ficers of the Regiment, and at the same time receive a severe re-primand from Col Phinney —

John Wales in Capt. Williams Company, Col Greaton Regiment

Issued at Cambridge, General George Washington's general orders for December 24, 1775, addressed recommendations for the rations of his troops. "As Milk cannot be procured during the Winter Season," wrote Washington, "The Men are to have . . . One Quart of Spruce Beer per day or nine Gallons of Molasses to one hundred Men per week." Library of Congress via author's collection

Below: *The kitchen was adjacent to the main house at Mount Vernon, as seen in this 1970 photograph, and it was used primarily for preparing food. However, George Washington almost certainly made forays into this structure to supervise the rolling boil of the wort that would become his legendary "small beer."* Library of Congress via author's collection

Above: *George Washington's grist mill near Mount Vernon was used to grind grain for bread and beer. The stone structure deteriorated in the century following Washington's passing, but it was finally restored in 1932.* Library of Congress via author's collection

TO MAKE SMALL BEER

By
George Washington

Though he favored the porter brewed by Robert Hare of Philadelphia, the "Father of Our Country" was also a noted home brewer in his own right, and he made sufficient quantities for his own use and for the entertainment of his guests. In his notebook for the year 1757, he jotted down this recipe for small beer:

> *Take a large Sifter full of Bran Hops to your Taste — Boil these 3 hours then strain out 30 Gallons. Into a Cooler put in 3 Gallons Molasses while the Beer is scalding hot or rather drain the molasses into the Cooler. Strain the Beer on it while boiling hot let this stand til it is little more than Blood warm. Then put in a quart of Yeast if the weather is very cold cover it over with a Blanket — & Let it work in the Cooler 24 hours then put it into the Cask — leave the Bung open til it is almost done working — Bottle it that day Week it was Brewed.*

By the 1760s, and probably sooner, bottled British porter began to be exported, first to Ireland and then to the American colonies. In Ireland, a number of brewers began making porter, not the least of whom was Arthur Guinness of the Saint James's Gate Brewery in Dublin. Guinness started brewing his legendary "stout porter" in about 1773. Saint James's Gate would later become, and remain so for about a century, the largest brewery in the world. Guinness Stout—often known in Ireland as

354.

of equal strength and of making the duty more equal in the detail of it. In a word many valuable advantages would result from it, whilst I can suggest but one reason against it (and that, fully satisfied I am, when weighed in the Scale of Interest, will not operate) I mean the keeping so many Officers in Camp, who might be spared from the duties of the Field till the Regiments are stronger than they are at present. The sixteen additional Regiments, labour under such disadvantages in some States, as to render the interposition of Congress (in some shape or other) indispensably necessary.

With respect to Food, considering we are in such an extensive and abundant Country, no Army was ever worse supplied than ours with many essential articles of it; our Soldiers, the greatest part of the last Campaign and the whole of this, have scarcely tasted any kind of vegetables, had but little Salt, and Vinegar which would have been a tolerable substitute for Vegetables, they have been in a great measure strangers to. Neither have they been provided with proper drink. Beer or Cyder seldom comes within the verge of the Camp, and Rum in much too small Quantities. Thus, to devouring large quantities of Animal Food, untempered by Vegetables, or Vinegar, or by any kind of Drink, but Water and eating indifferent Bread (but for this last a remedy is providing) are to be ascribed, the many putrid diseases incident to the Army, and the lamentable Mortality

Far Right: *General George Washington's letter to the Continental Congress Army Committee of July 19, 1777, states that his troops have not been "provided with proper drink. Beer or Cyder seldom comes within the verge of the Camp, and Rum in much too small quantities."* Library of Congress via author's collection

This mid-twentieth-century Kodachrome image depicts Thomas Jefferson's estate at Monticello in Albemarle County, Virginia. America's third president was the architect for the building and he supervised all functioning aspects of his adjacent property. Library of Congress via author's collection

"Guinness' Porter"—is still the world's definitive form of that beverage.

In America, Robert Hare began brewing porter in the auspicious year of 1776. Forced to temporarily abandon the city during the subsequent British occupation, Hare is said to have taken refuge in Virginia. It is possible that he may have had some contact during this time with George Washington, although the general would have been away fighting the Revolutionary War most of the time.

Washington had certainly become acquainted with Hare's porter by 1788, because on July 20 of that year he wrote to his deputy quartermaster general, Colonel Clement Biddle, "I beg you will send me a gross of Mr. Hairs best bottled Porter if the price is not much enhanced by the copious droughts you took of it at the late Procession." The "Procession" was possibly in reference to a victory parade.

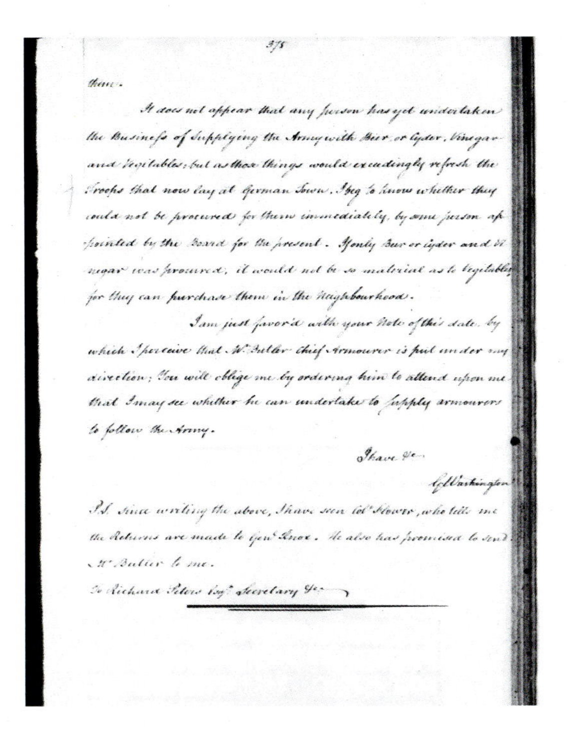

375

them.

It does not appear that any person has yet undertaken the Business of Supplying the Army with Beer or Cyder, Vinegar and Vegitables; but as those things would exceedingly refresh the Troops that now lay at German Town, I beg to know whether they could not be procured for them immediately, by some person appointed by the Board for the present. If only Beer or Cyder and Vinegar was procured, it would not be so material as to Vegitables for they can purchase them in the Neighbourhood.

I am just favor'd with your Note of this date, by which I perceive that Mr. Butler Chief Armourer is put under my direction; You will oblige me by ordering him to attend upon me that I may see whether he can undertake to supply armourers to follow the Army.

I have &c.

G. Washington

P.S. Since writing the above, I have seen Colo. Flower, who tells me the Returns are made to Genl. Knox. He also has promised to send Mr. Butler to me.

To Richard Peters Esqr. Secretary &c.

General George Washington's letter of August 5, 1777, notes "Beer, or Cyder, Vinegar and Vegetables . . . would exceedingly refresh the Troops. . . . If only Beer or Cyder and Vinegar was procured, it would not be so material as to Vegetables, for they can purchase them in the Neighbourhood." Library of Congress via author's collection

Structures such as the south service wing at Thomas Jefferson's Monticello housed a variety of activities related to the work of the estate. No doubt, casks of ale were fermented behind the stone walls. Library of Congress via author's collection

Right: *Issued at Lexington, General George Washington's general orders for January 26, 1778, stated, "The Commander in Chief is pleased to . . . order that" the troops should be provided with strong beer at two shillings and sixpence per quart and common beer at one shilling per quart.* Far right: *General George Washington was a constant champion of a beer ration for his troops. In his letter to Alexander Hamilton of May 2, 1783, he wrote, "If spruce, or any other kind of small Beer, could be provided, it ought to be given gratis, but not made part of the Compact with [the troops]."* Library of Congress via author's collection

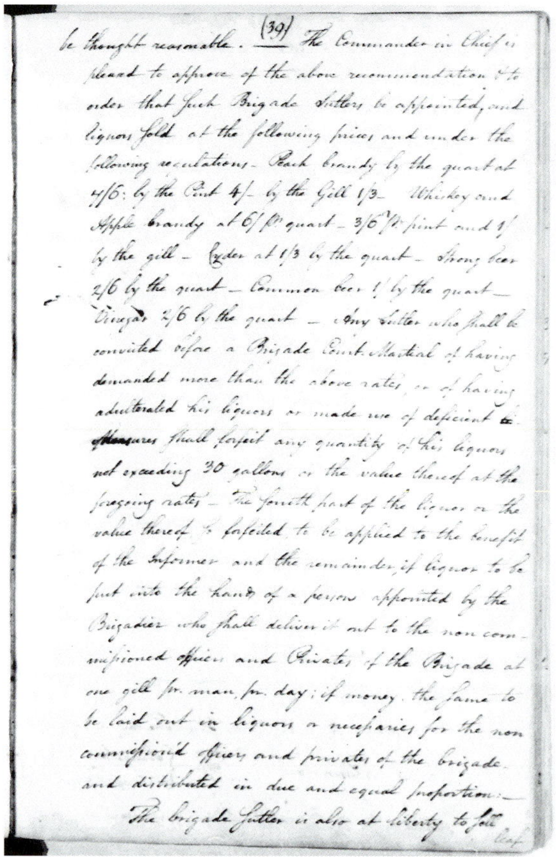

The adjective "best" clearly describes the president's opinion of Hare's product. Two years later, when Washington was at Federal Hall in New York, he asked his secretary, Tobias Lear, to place an order. Lear wrote, "Will you be so good as to desire Mr. Hare to have if he continues to make the best Porter in Philadelphia 3 gross of his best put up for Mount Vernon? as the President means to visit that place in the recess of Congress and it is probable there will be a large demand for Porter at that time."

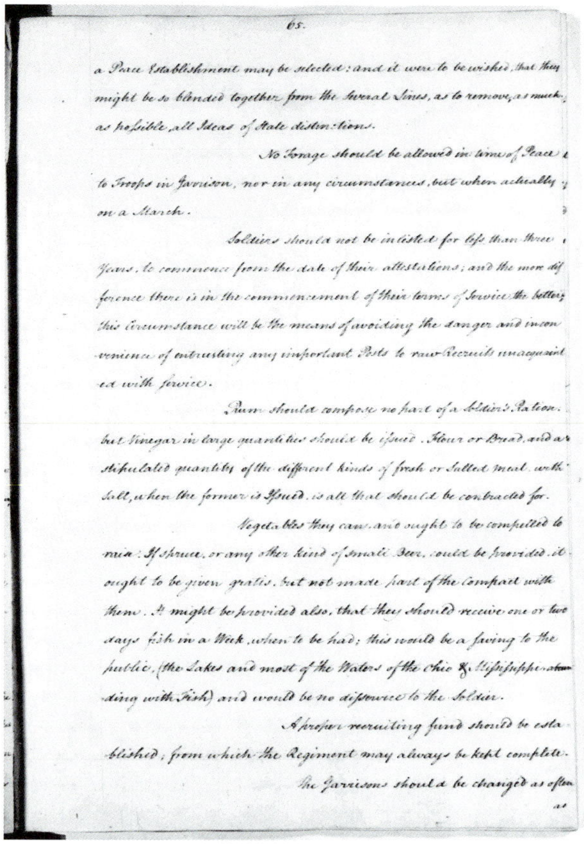

A receipt issued to Washington and his entourage in July 1782 by George Evans at Philadelphia's City Tavern gives us further insight into the general's eating and drinking habits. In addition to listing three dinners on July 21, five breakfasts on July 23, and two breakfasts and four "gentleman's breakfasts" on July 24, it states, "There were punch and beverages, beer and cider and three bottles of wine for the sick included."

While he was at home in Mount Vernon in the quieter years before the war and his presidency, Washington had brewed his own beer. The fact that his recipe for "small beer" (see sidebar) discusses thirty-gallon quantities indicates that he was brewing for more than just his own personal use.

For Washington, porter also had a political dimension. After the war, the first president was a champion of the notion that Americans should buy the products of American manufacturers, rather than goods imported from England. Porter was specifically mentioned. Washington was quick to point out that he bought only "American porter" and asked that his fellow countrymen follow his example.

During the Revolutionary War, Washington was a constant champion of the beer ration that he felt his men deserved. One finds repeated references to beer and the beer ration in his personal papers, which are preserved in the Library of Congress and elsewhere. For example, on July 19, 1777, General Washington wrote to the Continental Congress Army Committee, stating, "With respect to Food, considering we are in such an extensive and abundant Country, No Army was ever worse supplied than ours with many essential Articles of it. Our Soldiers, the greatest part of the last Campaign, and the whole of this, have scarcely tasted any kind of Vegetables, had but little Salt, and Vinegar. . . . Neither have they been provided with proper drink. Beer or Cyder seldom comes within the verge of the Camp, and Rum in much too small quantities."

On July 25, Congress resolved that the committee should be empowered to contract for, among other things, "beer, cider and sauerkraut."

A few weeks later, on August 5, 1777, Washington wrote to the Continental Congress War Board that "It does not appear that any person has yet undertaken the Business of Supplying the Army with Beer, or Cyder, Vinegar and Vegetables; but as those things would exceedingly refresh the Troops that now lay at German Town, I beg to know whether they could not be procured for them immediately, by some person appointed by the Board for the present. If only Beer or Cyder and Vinegar was procured, it would not be so material as to Vegetables, for they can purchase them in the Neighbourhood."

On wintry January 26, 1778, Washington's general orders for the day stated, "The Commander in Chief is pleased to . . . order that . . . [a] Brigade Sutler be appointed, and liquors sold at the following prices and under the following regulations: Peach brandy by the quart at 7/6 by the Pint 4/, by the Gill 1/3. Whiskey and Apple brandy at 6/ pr. quart, 3/6 pr. pint and 1/ by the gill. Cyder at 1/3 by the quart; Strong beer 2/6 by the quart. Common beer 1/ by the quart." The prices are in schillings and pence.

General Washington eventually decided that the Continental Army should underwrite the cost of beer for the troops. In a letter to Alexander Hamilton, penned on May 2, 1783, he wrote, "If spruce, or any other kind of small Beer, could be provided, it ought to be given gratis, but not made part of the Compact with [the troops]."

Thomas Jefferson was a true Renaissance man; he was an architect, statesman, and philosopher who also maintained vineyards and a brewhouse on his estate. After serving as the third president of the United States, Jefferson was approached by Joseph Coppinger to aid in a scheme to establish a United States National Brewery. Library of Congress via author's collection

The personal papers and correspondence of Thomas Jefferson, like those of George Washington, contain many references to beer and brewing. Both men made note of buying beer, and both favored Philadelphia brewers. For Jefferson, it was a man named Henry Pepper, who had emigrated from Germany as Heinrich Pfeiffer and had anglicized his name. During the 1790s, Jefferson was a regular patron of Pepper's brewery on Fifth Street.

While George Washington's interest in the brewer's art preceded the Revolutionary War and his presidency, Jefferson's appears to have come later in life. Whereas Washington favored porter and brewed small ale for his household use, the more inquisitive Jefferson was more eclectic when it came to beer-making. In addition to his experiments with corn, rather than barley, as a fermentable starch in some of his beer, we know from his letters that he also brewed wheat beer at his estate at Monticello.

It was shortly after he left office that Jefferson happened to cross paths with a man named Joseph

Beer is delivered to Fraunces Tavern on Pearl Street in New York City. Etienne Delancey constructed the three-story building in 1719, and it was purchased by Samuel Fraunces and opened as the Queen's Head Tavern in 1762. Beer was almost certainly produced on the premises before the Revolutionary War. In 1783, as the war came to a close, one of the tavern's patrons, General George Washington, hosted his officers in a victory banquet here. On December 4, Washington made his famous farewell speech here. After the war, Fraunces housed some of the Continental Congress offices as the Articles of Confederation were written. The site continued to function as a tavern through the nineteenth and twentieth centuries. Library of Congress via author's collection

Coppinger, one of the most interesting characters in the early brewing history of the United States. Coppinger was a self-styled "Porter Brewer from Europe" who had first drifted onto the American brewing scene at Pittsburgh in about 1802. For about a year he was a partner, along with Peter Shiras, in Pittsburgh's Point Brewery. Then he pulled out inexplicably and moved to New York. Over the next few years his peculiar crusade began to take shape.

Coppinger was one of those energetic dreamers and entrepreneurs who would help shape America's

Right: *The manner in which the large structure on the left is set back from the road suggests that Miller's Tavern maintained a large commercial brewery at one time. One can imagine casks being rolled into wagons at this loading dock before the tree was planted. Located at Copake in the Hudson River Valley of New York, the tavern is said to have been frequented by former president and former New York governor Martin van Buren. Also known through the years as Deyo's Tavern and the Quackenbush Tavern, the building was built sometime before 1835. When photographed on October 1, 1936, it appeared to have been a private home.* Library of Congress via author's collection

future. He had a dream that the United States ought to have a National Brewery. By this, he did not mean a brewery that was national in the way that Adolphus Busch would later dream of a national brewery; he intended a National Brewery similar to the new nation's Army, Navy, Post Office, and Supreme Court.

On December 16, 1810, the porter brewer from Europe sat down at his desk and outlined his plan in a personal letter to President James Madison, which is still preserved in the Library of Congress:

> *I am not fortunate enough to have it in my power to interest wealthy and influential characters in the request I am about to make to you. Still I am not without hopes of ultimate success in calling your attention to what I have long had earnestly at heart, that is the establishment of a Brewing Company at Washington as a national object. It has in my view the greatest importance as it would unquestionably tend to improve the quality of our Malt Liquors in every part of the Union and serve to counteract the baneful influence of ardent spirits on the health and morals of our fellow citizens.*

Coppinger went on to remind Madison of the profitability of the major breweries in the United Kingdom, which then included Bass and Guinness. Coppinger suggested that the United States National Brewery could be put into operation for $20,000, a sum to be raised by the sale of bonds of $500 and $1,000. He went on to promise Madison a 200 percent profit on the sale of ale and porter in bottles.

Five days later, Coppinger wrote another letter to the president in which he underscored the

Built in 1792 by Captain John Chisholm, the Chisholm Tavern at Front and Gay Streets is said to have been the first hotel in Knoxville, Tennessee. At the time, eastern Tennessee was considered to be the Far West, the edge of civilization, so beer brewed in the East was hard to import. The tavern needed beer, and brewing almost certainly took place in one of the buildings seen here. Still standing, it was nevertheless a shadow of its former glory when it was photographed in April 1934. Library of Congress via author's collection

George Hitchner constructed the Alloway Tavern at Main and Greenwich Streets in Alloway, New Jersey, between 1820 and 1826. It was eventually sold to Samuel Dare in 1838. When this photograph was taken in April 1937, draft beer was served, but it was almost certainly no longer being brewed here. Library of Congress via author's collection

Left: *Smoke still curled from the chimney when the Nixon Tavern on Fairchance Road in Fayette County, Pennsylvania, was photographed during a snowy March in 1934. Some records indicate that the building may have been constructed in 1810, although other sources suggest that Hananiah Davis held a deed to the property as early as 1770. It is said that she was in partnership with Moses Nixon at the tavern in 1835, some 65 years later. One of the more colorful tales about the tavern dates back to 1810. The bandit Phillip Rogers murdered young Polly Williams in the nearby White Rocks Mountains and brought her body to the tavern to keep it there overnight.* Library of Congress via author's collection

notion that "those families who are in the custom of using malt liquor freely as their common drink all summer, keep and preserve their health while their less fortunate neighbors who are deprived of it are the victims of fever and disease."

The record shows that Madison passed Coppinger's communiqués on to former President Jefferson for his comments. Jefferson considered the matter, but before anything substantial could be undertaken, the United States found itself embroiled in the chaos of the War of 1812.

Right: *John Chandler opened The Bonney Tavern, a roadhouse located on the Daniel Webster Highway in Merrimack County, New Hampshire, in 1787, one year before New Hampshire was inducted into statehood. The structure that probably served as a brewhouse is clearly visible in the rear. Also known as the Penacook House, the establishment no doubt maintained a brewhouse because it was a long, rough drive from regional brewing centers such as Boston in the late eighteenth century. This photo was taken shortly before the historic roadhouse was demolished in 1937.* Library of Congress via author's collection

The Zoar Society Brewery was constructed in 1830 in the village of Zoar in Tuscarawas County, Ohio. The people of Zoar were German immigrants who had broken with the established Lutheran church and left Germany to escape persecution for their religious beliefs. They established their community along the Tuscarawas River in the 1820s, and they soon built their own brewery. The settlers called their settlement Zoar, after Lot's Biblical town of refuge. Library of Congress via author's collection

Though the Zoar Society Brewery building was still in good repair when it was photographed in December 1936, the fermentation cellar downstairs had clearly not been used for some time. The Zoar Society remained isolated from mainstream Ohio until the 1880s; with the arrival of railroad links to the outside world, the community gradually dissolved. It was officially disbanded in 1898, although many structures at the site survived. Library of Congress via author's collection

In 1815, as the war drew to a close, Coppinger published his book, *The American Brewer & Maltster's Assistant*, which included a section on brewing beer with Indian corn. The book is known to have caught Jefferson's fancy, and letters preserved in the Library of Congress indicate that the former president wrote to bookstores inquiring about Coppinger's volume even before it was published.

His book completed, Coppinger once again turned to his National Brewery idea. On April 6, 1815, he again raised the idea with Jefferson, hoping to enlist the support of the elder statesman. On April 25, Jefferson responded, "I have no doubt, either in a moral or economical view, of the desirableness to introduce a taste for malt liquors instead of that for ardent spirits. . . . The business of brewing is now so much introduced in every state, that it appears to me to need no other encouragement than to increase the number of customers. I do not think it a case where a company need form itself merely on patriotic principles, because there is a sufficiency of private capital which would embark itself in the business if there were a demand."

Jefferson went on to say that he considered himself "too old and too fond of quiet" to get involved in the scheme. He mentioned to Coppinger—brewer to brewer—that he was now brewing wheat beer at Monticello, and he closed in wishing the porter brewer from Europe a hearty "best wishes."

Essentially, Jefferson had told him that it was a good idea, but that there was no reason for the government to get involved when there were enough commercial breweries sprouting up in the land—and for Coppinger not to bother him any more.

It is intriguing to imagine what might have happened if Jefferson *had* been interested. What if

Patrons enjoy a few pints at an early nineteenth-century tavern. The man in the center whispers confidences to the patient hostess who has just refilled his glass from a porcelain pitcher. Note that the men are drinking from glassware, while older style tankards, perhaps belonging to regular patrons, hang from the wall. Author's collection

Jefferson had supported and championed the idea? Could Thomas Jefferson have reentered public service as our first Brewmaster General? We have Alexander Hamilton, the first Secretary of the Treasury, pictured on the ten-dollar bill. Imagine Thomas Jefferson on 11-ounce, government-issue bottles.

While Washington and Jefferson probably brewed significant quantities of beer in their day, both were merely gentleman brewers. They were in it for the beer, not to create an economically viable venture. Another important name in early American history was, coincidentally, a commercial brewer. Matthew Vassar is best known today for endowing the college in Poughkeepsie, New York, which bears his name.

Matthew's father, James Vassar, was a homebrewer who went commercial around 1801. His customer base included wagon stops along the Hudson River from Poughkeepsie to New York City. The business flourished, and in 1810 Matthew and his brother took over the business.

When the original brewery burned a year later, young Matthew, just a lad of nineteen years, established a brewpub and tavern in the basement of a courthouse. In the building of a business, it is said that the three most important things are "location, location, location." Vassar's choice would certainly have been good for *re*building a business. In 1813, Matthew Vassar rebuilt the family brewery at Poughkeepsie and added a second brewing plant in 1832. Vassar was active in the business until after the Civil War, and at that time he was brewing 30,000 barrels of beer annually.

COLONIAL BEER STYLES

Typically, eighteenth-century English and colonial beer would have been ale, *an amber-colored, lightly hopped, bottom-fermenting beer similar to English ale of today. The shade of the amber color was relative to the extent to which the malted barley was roasted.*

While barley is the definitive malting grain in beer-making, the English occasionally used oats, and the American colonists are known to have experimented with corn and wheat.

Ale was occasionally flavored as in the Belgian-style fruit beers. Letters and documents dating from the colonial period indicate that eighteenth-century brewers experimented with apple and pumpkin beer.

India Pale Ale *was invented by English brewers specifically to be exported to English colonists in India. It was lighter in malt content and hence lighter in color than the average ale, accounting for the term "Pale." Meanwhile, it was much more heavily hopped than typical ale. The extra hops were added as a preservative to help sustain the beer for the long journey to India, as well as while it was stored in India. Refrigeration, other than to pack something in ice, did not, of course, exist in the eighteenth century. India Pale Ale was also exported to the American colonies.*

Porter, *which become instantly popular after its invention in 1722, was a dark, creamy, bottom-fermented beer made with darkly roasted malt.*

Small beer *was a term widely used in the eighteenth and nineteenth centuries to describe a low-alcohol ale typically brewed at home and consumed relatively soon after it was brewed. Presumably, if left to ferment longer, it would mature into what would have been described in the terminology of the era as* table beer *or* strong beer.

Lager, *a top-fermenting beer, was starting to become popular in continental Europe, but it was not so in England and is not noted to have appeared in America until the second quarter of the nineteenth century.*

Just as Joseph Coppinger was the archetypal dreamer of big ideas, Vassar was the model of a successful early-nineteenth-century entrepreneur. In addition to his brewing operations, he acquired farmland as far away as Wisconsin in order to control his own supply of hops. After his retirement, his company continued to produce beer until 1895.

Though the Vassar Brewery was one of the largest great English-style breweries in America at the beginning of the nineteenth century, a contemporary upstart in rural Pennsylvania eclipsed its longevity. In 1829, David G. Yuengling, a brewer from the German state of Wurtemburg, arrived in the Schuylkill County village of Pottsville. There, in the Appalachian foothills, Yuengling established what he called—with a nod to a familiar patriotic symbol—the Eagle Brewery. Whereas Vassar's operation was a fading memory by the dawn of the twentieth century, Yuengling's brewery would still be going strong in the twenty-first century. When Yuengling's second son, Frederick, took over in 1873, the company was renamed D.G. Yuengling & Son. Under this name it survives to this day, still under family ownership, as the oldest brewery in the United States.

When David Yuengling started his business in 1829, one of his staple products was, naturally, porter. This beverage would gradually fade into obscurity in the twentieth century. However, the Yuengling brewery would remain as one of the only porter brewers in the United States in the decades leading up to the Microbrewery Revolution of the 1980s.

By the time David Yuengling stirred his first batch of wort in Pottsville, the brewing industry in the United States had matured and was suffering through a general decline in per capita beer consumption. However, as students of economic cycles know, everything swings on a pendulum. The decline of the industry in the 1820s and 1830s only set the stage for an event of truly enormous proportions—the Lager Revolution.

The Germans were coming.

AMER CAN BREWER
NO PARKING

By the 1820s, the per capita consumption of English beer styles in the United States had started to wane. French wine, always popular on the tables of the gentry, was more widely available than ever, as was Caribbean rum. Meanwhile, whiskey was also becoming increasingly popular. The Whiskey Rebellion of 1794 had been about taxation, with the people living west of the Appalachians insisting that they would not be taken advantage of by the more populous East. The fact that whiskey was the centerpiece of the rebellion illustrates how important the small distillers in the West had become to the national economy.

By the late 1820s, the West was emerging as an important part of the United States, not merely an incidental anteroom to the long-established coastal civilization. The election in 1828 of the first Western president of the United States, Andrew "Old Hickory" Jackson of Tennessee, was one indication of the cultural shift. The rise of corn whiskey from Tennessee and Kentucky was another.

On the technical side, the westerners had discovered that the abundant surplus of corn was much more useful in distilling than in brewing. In addition, whiskey was far less prone to spoilage than beer—the latter has a shelf life of a few months under the best of conditions, while whiskey, like wine, improves with age and can be stored for years.

Coincidentally, the beer that revived the brewing industry in America takes its name from the German word meaning "to store." *Lager* beer is chemically very distinct from English ale or porter. Whereas the latter beers are made with yeast that ferments on top of the fermenting vessel, lager yeast sinks to the bottom.

Opposite: *Architectural historians called the Wiessner Brewery (a.k.a. American Brewery) in Baltimore one of the finest examples of the "Teutonic Brewery" style of architecture. The people in northeast Baltimore called it the "Germanic Pagoda." Brewing began here in 1887 and continued until 1973, two years after this photograph was taken.* Library of Congress via author's collection

Right: *Jacob Best brought lager brewing to Milwaukee. He arrived in 1844 and opened his Empire Brewery, in the process becoming the patriarch of a dynasty that would make the city famous as a brewing center.* Far Right: *Philip Best was one of Jacob Best's sons. Together with his brother, Charles, he was an important member of the second generation of Milwaukee brewers. Philip's daughter married Frederick Pabst.* Author illustrations

Lager is also fermented at much colder temperatures, and brewers "store" or "lager" it in the fermenters for a much longer period of time.

Lager was invented in the mountains of Central Europe, roughly in the region that now comprises Austria, the German state of Bavaria, and the Czech state of Bohemia. Lager was first brewed commercially in 1840 by the Spaten Brewery in Munich and by the Schwechat Brewery in Vienna, both of which are still in business today. Two years later, brewers in the Pilsen region of Bohemia started brewing a lighter lager that they dubbed "pilsner" to distinguish it from the more amber Munich and Vienna lagers. Today, the original pilsner brewery in Pilsen still markets its lager worldwide under the brand name "Pilsner Urquell," meaning "the original Pilsner."

There were some German immigrants to America in the colonial period, and many of them were brewers. Lager did not reach the New World until 1840, the same year that commercial production began in Europe. Around that time, a great influx of immigrants from the economically troubled, patchwork German principalities began arriving in the United States.

According to the best evidence, lager yeast first arrived in the United States in the possession of a man named John (Johann) Wagner. A former brewmaster from Bavaria, Wagner immigrated to Philadelphia and set up a small brewery on Poplar Street. Over the next several years, lager brewing gradually gained a foothold in the city. Wagner shared his yeast with his friend George Manger, who started a brewery on Second Street. Next came Charles (Karl) Wolf, Manger's former employer. A former German brewer, Wolf had started a sugar refinery in Philadelphia, but when he got his hands on lager yeast, he promptly returned to his former profession.

By the time Wolf opened his brewery on Dillwyn Street in 1844, lager brewing had spread from Philadelphia to cities such as New York and Cincinnati, where there were sizable German communities. More importantly, it was not only the Germans who found themselves enjoying a glass of lager. Drinking of the golden brew also soon expanded beyond the German immigrant enclaves to the rest of the population. Descendants of English colonists, who had eschewed their grandfathers' porter in favor of whiskey and rum, quickly developed a taste for the cold beverage from Bavaria.

The social and economic upheaval in Europe during the 1840s—especially in the patchwork of German-speaking principalities in 1848—turned the trickle of German immigration to America into a flood. Awaiting the immigrants was not only a handful of lager brewers, but profitable business opportunities for would-be lager brewers. Though lager was by then universally favored, it was nearly always brewed by the hands of Germans. For the next century, German immigrants and their families would dominate 90 percent of the brewing industry in the United States.

Everywhere that the new German immigrants congregated, a lager brewery was soon established. In Cincinnati, for example, the first lager brewer is said to have been Franz Fortmann, who took over the Agneil & Fleishman Bavarian Brewery in 1844.

In New York, which had alternated with Philadelphia as the brewing capital of the United States since before there was a United States, lager breweries and German *biergartens,* or "beer gardens," proliferated. The first may have been George Gillig, although he had some early competition from Frederick and Maximilian Schaefer, whose surname would become a household word among New York beer lovers for more than a century.

In Baltimore, where English-style breweries had existed for a century, George (Georg) Rossmarck began brewing lager in 1846. He was soon followed by Frederick Ludwig in 1848 and by George Rost in 1849. Rost's operation evolved into the Bismarck Brewing Company, which survived until 1940; both Rossmarck's and Ludwig's breweries were closed by the end of the nineteenth century. One of the city's most interesting lager brewers—especially for the architectural legacy he left to Baltimore—was John (Johann) Frederick Wiessner. Although he was a latecomer to the Lager Revolution, arriving during the Civil War, he bequeathed the city an architectural landmark that is clearly a symbol of the lager movement. Wiessner began brewing in 1863 on North Gay Street, but he is best remembered for the grand brewery he built on the same site in 1887. The flamboyant architecture made it what architectural historians once called one of the finest examples of the "Teutonic Brewery" style in the United States. It was certainly a landmark in northeast Baltimore, where it was referred to as the "Germanic Pagoda." After Wiessner died in 1897, the company remained a Baltimore landmark. It would emerge from Prohibition as American Brewing and continue operating until 1973.

A vintage nineteenth-century mechanism for milling malt and typical of a smaller brewery of the period. This machine would have had a capacity equal to the amount of malt necessary for a single batch. Bill Yenne

Charles Best started the Plank Road Brewery in 1850 in the Milwaukee suburb of Wauwatosa. Several years later, Frederick Miller acquired the property and it became the cornerstone of his growing empire. In 1985, the Miller Brewing Company revived the "Plank Road" brand name. Miller Brewing Company via author's collection

Right: *Frederick Miller was a German who learned the brewer's trade in France. After a stint as a house brewer for the Hohenzollerns, he immigrated to the United States and settled in Milwaukee in 1855. His company evolved into one of America's largest brewers.* Author illustration

The Lager Revolution served to abruptly reverse the decline in per capita consumption of beer that had begun around 1820. Whereas in colonial times, one might have two or three pints in a sitting—and usually *not* on Sunday—lager drinkers at the German biergartens consumed considerably more—and often on Sunday. An 1850 lithograph depicting a biergarten includes a sign limiting patrons to "48 glasses."

Much to the chagrin of the descendants of the Puritans, the newer Americans insisted that lager was not actually an intoxicating beverage—which of course was not actually true. An October 1885 article in *Harper's Monthly* recalls, "During a famous trial some years since, soon after lager found its way to America, evidence was introduced to show that the beverage was not intoxicating. Old-time imbibers one after another testified as to capacity of stomach and steadiness of head, until the climax

Micheli's 7 Mile House was a roadhouse typical of the nineteenth-century American West. Naturally, beer was served, and because the roadhouse was located in San Francisco, steam beer was the specific style. Steam beer was first created during the Gold Rush era by fermenting lager yeast at ale temperatures. San Francisco History Center via author's collection

Far Left: *Between 1897 and the eve of Prohibition, the North Star Brewing Company operated on Army Street in the Mission District of San Francisco. A company with offices on Sansome Street briefly revived the brand name after Prohibition.*
Left: *Jacob Adams started his Broadway Brewery at 637 Broadway in San Francisco in 1874. The company moved to Nineteenth Street in the Mission District in 1895, but folded in 1916 before the enactment of Prohibition.*

This view of the boiler exteriors at the Wiessner Brewery in Baltimore displays both nineteenth-century workmanship and nineteenth-century decorative ideals. The Wiessner facility began using steam to heat its mash at a time when many rival breweries were still using direct heat. Library of Congress via author's collection

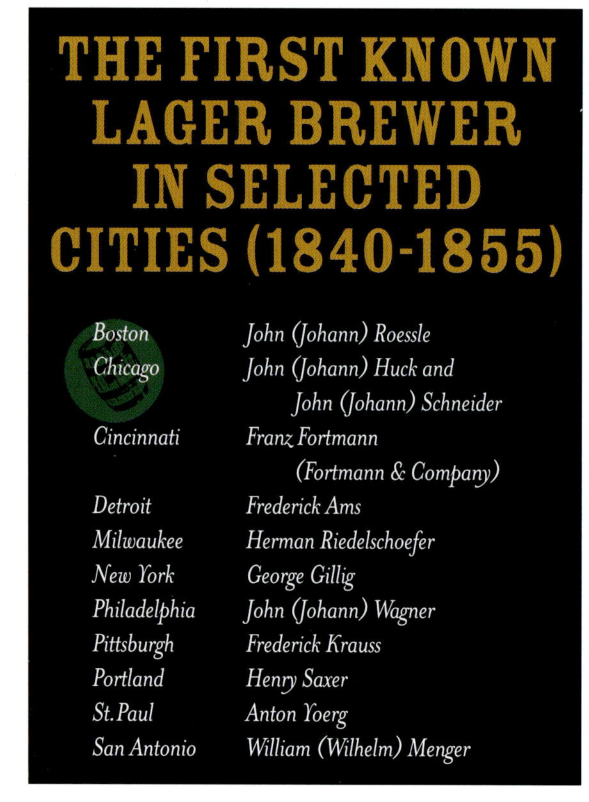

THE FIRST KNOWN LAGER BREWER IN SELECTED CITIES (1840-1855)

City	Brewer
Boston	*John (Johann) Roessle*
Chicago	*John (Johann) Huck and John (Johann) Schneider*
Cincinnati	*Franz Fortmann (Fortmann & Company)*
Detroit	*Frederick Ams*
Milwaukee	*Herman Riedelschoefer*
New York	*George Gillig*
Philadelphia	*John (Johann) Wagner*
Pittsburgh	*Frederick Krauss*
Portland	*Henry Saxer*
St. Paul	*Anton Yoerg*
San Antonio	*William (Wilhelm) Menger*

was reached in a worthy descendant of old King Cole, who claimed an ability to dispose of 60 glasses at a single sitting. The advocates of total abstinence stood aghast at the disclosure, while even the moderate drinkers retreated in disorder."

Though the rapidly expanding lager industry would eventually eclipse the declining market for ale, brewers of the latter continued to be an important factor in the United States until the Civil War. In Chicago, when John (Johann) Huck and John (Johann) Schneider arrived in 1847 to set up their lager business, they faced stiff competition from the Lill & Diversey ale brewery. Founded by William Lill in 1833, Lill & Diversey has been described as the largest brewery in the West in the decades leading up to the Civil War. Records show that Lill and his partner, Michael Diversey, distributed their ale and porter northwest as far as St. Paul, northeast to Buffalo, and down the Mississippi as far as New Orleans. Until the eve of the Civil War, when exports to the South ended abruptly, the output of the Lill & Diversey enterprise was nearly 45,000 barrels annually.

Between Chicago and New Orleans lay another city that would soon emerge as a major inland brewing center. St. Louis had been a major trading post on the Mississippi River for nearly a century when Thomas Biddle established his Phoenix Brewery there in about 1825. A generation later, the Germans arrived. It marked an auspicious moment in 1852 when George Schneider started brewing lager in St. Louis. His brewery, which was known as the Bavarian Brewery from 1856 to 1875, would later be taken over by Eberhard Anheuser. In turn, Anheuser brought his ambitious son-in-law, Adolphus Busch, into the business.

The Germans also arrived in Texas at about this time, and San Antonio rapidly became a major center of German-American culture. In 1855, Wilhelm—later William—Menger became the first commercial lager brewer in the Lone Star State when he started his Western Brewery on Blum Street in San Antonio. After the Civil War, San Antonio would emerge as the brewing capital of the former Confederacy.

Above: *This photo provides a detailed view of a governor among the industrial equipment at the Wiessner Brewery in Baltimore. Used in pumps for this application, a governor is a device used to maintain uniform speed regardless of load changes, usually by regulating the supply of fuel or hydraulic fluid.* Library of Congress via author's collection

Colorado's first brewery, the Rocky Mountain Brewery, was opened in Denver in 1859, a year after the Colorado Gold Rush began. As elsewhere during this era, the proprietors were German—Charles (Karl) Tascher and F.Z. Solomon.

While New York and Philadelphia had long been peerless in their claims to the title, it was with the Lager Revolution that Milwaukee, Wisconsin, began to see the rise of the industry that would make it the brewing capital of the United States after the Civil War. Milwaukee was a young city when the Lager Revolution came to American shores. It was formed in 1838 through the consolidation of several fur-trading settlements, although it was not officially incorporated as a city until 1846. In the meantime, not one but *three* breweries were established in Milwaukee in 1840, coincidentally the same year that John (Johann) Wagner first brought lager yeast to America.

Right: *During the nineteenth century and well into the twentieth, beer was transported and stored in wooden kegs that weighed about 100 pounds when empty. Like wine or whiskey barrels, the kegs were made of oak. Wooden beer kegs, however, can be distinguished by the fact that they are more heavily banded, because beer, unlike other beverages, continues to increase in pressure after the container is filled.*

Because of the nascent city's far remove from the East Coast where lager yeast was introduced that year, the first of Milwaukee's brewhouses was an ale and porter brewery. Known as the Milwaukee Brewery, this establishment was started on Huron Street by a partnership of three Welshmen: John Davis, Richard Owens, and William Pawlett. The trio not only brewed ale and porter, but they also distilled whiskey. According to the city's official history, the men started brewing with a five-barrel capacity, but imported a 40-barrel copper brew kettle from Chicago in 1844.

The first lager brewer in Milwaukee was probably Herman Reuthlisberger (a.k.a. Riedelschoefer) in 1840. He named his new facility on Virginia Street the German Brewery, apparently to underscore the fact that he was brewing lager and the Milwaukee was not. A year later, Riedelschoefer sold his business to J.R. Maier, who renamed it the Lake Brewery. Maier, in turn, sold out to Franz Neukirch in 1844. In 1848, Neukirch took on a partner, C.J. Melms, whose family would continue to run the business as the Menominee Brewery until 1869.

The third brewery to open its doors in Milwaukee in 1840 was Stotz & Krill on Ogden Street. The following year, the Eagle Brewery (not to be confused with David G. Yuengling's brewery, founded in 1829) opened on Prairie Street, and in 1843, William Pawlett, late of the Milwaukee Brewery, bought into the business. In 1842, the Munzinger & Koethe Brewery opened on Burrell Street, rounding out the first generation of Milwaukee breweries.

David Gipfel constructed his first lager brewery in Milwaukee in 1843. Six years later, ownership passed to Karl Wilhelm (Charles) Gipfel, possibly David's son. Charles operated the company under the name Union Brewery, and in

A vintage nineteenth-century keg capper. The lever allowed the worker to force the cap into the bunghole with sufficient force so that it would resist the increasing pressure created by the unpasteurized beer as it continued to ferment inside the keg. The pressure gauge was used at the brewery to observe the progress of the fermentation by monitoring pressure.

A typical Old West brewery, the Union Brewery in Virginia City, Nevada, was founded in 1866 as the first brewery in Virginia City and one of the first in the state. There would be a proliferation of other breweries in the city during the Comstock Boom a decade later, but none except Union would survive Prohibition. Union was still serving its signature Tahoe brand when this photo was taken in 1937. A half-century later, a modern brewpub called Union Brewery opened here. Library of Congress via author's collection

1853 he built a brewery building on Chestnut Street (later Juneau Avenue) that would be recognized a century later as the oldest standing brewhouse in the state of Wisconsin. Herman Schliebitz, who operated the company between 1892 and 1894 as the Weiss Beer Brewery was the last brewer on the site.

The first of the legendary Milwaukee brewing families was established in 1844 when Jacob Best opened his Empire Brewery on Chestnut Street. His sons, especially Charles and Phillip, would go on to be the men who helped "make Milwaukee famous." Charles would start the company that evolved into Miller Brewing, while Phillip's daughter would marry a steamship captain named Frederick Pabst.

While Phillip—originally in partnership with brother Jacob Jr.—stayed to take over the family business in 1853, Charles struck out on his own. In 1850, he started the Menominee Valley Brewery, or the Plank Road Brewery, in nearby Wauwatosa. The latter name was a reference to the

In 1853, Karl Wilhelm (Charles) Gipfel constructed this building on West Juneau Avenue in Milwaukee as that city's Union Brewery. A century later the building was recognized as the oldest standing brewhouse in Wisconsin. It was last used as a brewery in 1894; during the 1920s, when this photo was taken, the building housed the Elsner Harness Shop. Library of Congress via author's collection

This Lager bier poster, dating from about 1879, was clearly designed to influence public perception of lager drinking. While the character in the center is a bit intimidating, the illustrations on the sides show lager as a staple of American life. To picture it as a "Family Drink" was in direct contrast to contemporary temperance posters. Library of Congress via author's collection

Top right: *H. & J. Pfaff began brewing lager in 1857 at Pynchon and Arch Streets in Roxbury, Boston. In this strange illustration, Joseph Jefferson, the stage actor famed for his portrayal of Rip Van Winkle, is seated on a keg being pulled by goats and escorted by satyrs. Goats are emblematic of bock beer, a Germanic lager style.* Library of Congress via author's collection

practice of using wood to pave the streets in timber-rich Wisconsin. Charles' brother Lorenz joined him briefly in 1851, but several years later, they closed their doors.

In 1854 (some sources say that it was in 1853), the brewery was reopened by a young German immigrant whose anglicized name was Frederick Edward John Miller. The brewery's name changed to Miller Brewing, although the company would revive the "Plank Road Brewery" name in 1985 for specialty products. Born in 1824, Frederick Miller was a member of an influential family from Riedlingen, in the southern German state of Wurtemburg. From the age of 14, however, he lived in France, and he apprenticed as a brewer at a brewery owned by his uncle in the Lorraine city of Nancy. He later re-crossed the Rhine to take over operations at the Royal Hohenzollern brewery in Sigmaringen.

In 1854, Miller and his wife, Josephine, came to the United States with a sizable nest egg that is mentioned in some accounts to have been a gift from the Hohenzollern family.

After living briefly in New York City, the Millers and their young son, Joseph, relocated to Milwaukee, where Frederick acquired the Plank Road Brewery. Company records indicate that he brewed his first batch of beer in 1855, and a newspaper account noted that he opened a beer hall on East Water Street in Milwaukee in 1857.

Life in Milwaukee was not easy for Frederick Miller. He and his wife lost several children in infancy, and in April 1860, Josephine passed away as well. She may have died in childbirth, or perhaps from cholera, which was claiming more than sixty people a week in the area.

To complicate matters, the Civil War began in 1861 and negatively impacted Miller's business. Later

A German immigrant in a jaunty, feathered hat displays a wide grin as he sits down to enjoy his beer. The porcelain stein is certainly characteristic of Germany and Central Europe, but by the middle of the nineteenth century, the steins were being made in America. Author's collection

in 1860, Miller married Lisette Gross. They had several children, five of whom survived to form the progenitors of the Miller family that would control Frederick Miller's company until it was sold to the W.R. Grace Company in 1966. In 1970, the Philip Morris tobacco company assumed full control of Miller.

Farther west, on the banks of the Mississippi, were the Twin Cities in what would in 1858 become the state of Minnesota. In 1848, Anton Yoerg started what was probably the first brewery in the future capital city of St. Paul on South Washington Street. Through 1855, the City Brewery, the North Star Brewery, the North Mississippi Brewery, and the Fleckenstein Brothers Brewery joined Yoerg's establishment on the roster of breweries. In 1860, Andrew Keller opened his Pittsburgh Brewery in St. Paul; before the Civil War was over, a man named Theodore Hamm would own it.

Across the river from St. Paul, in Minneapolis, both Gottlieb Gluek and John (Johann) Orth founded breweries in the 1850s. Orth's company, later known as Minneapolis Brewing & Malting, would always be best known by the brand name of its flagship lager—Grain Belt.

In the 1840s and 1850s, cities such as Milwaukee and St. Paul were America's western frontier. The virtually unpopulated territories west of the Mississippi were another world. The three Pacific Coast states were not even possessions of the United States when Jacob Best started brewing on Chestnut Street in 1844, although a majority of the population "out West" comprised American citizens.

On the Pacific Coast, Oregon, comprising the modern states of Oregon and Washington, was not chartered as a territory until 1846. California had briefly declared itself a republic in 1846 with the aid of United States forces, and Mexico formally ceded the territory to the United States in 1848. California would become a state in 1850, and Oregon would follow in 1859. By this time, both states had a thoroughly evolved brewing history.

The history of California in the nineteenth century is defined primarily by a single event—the

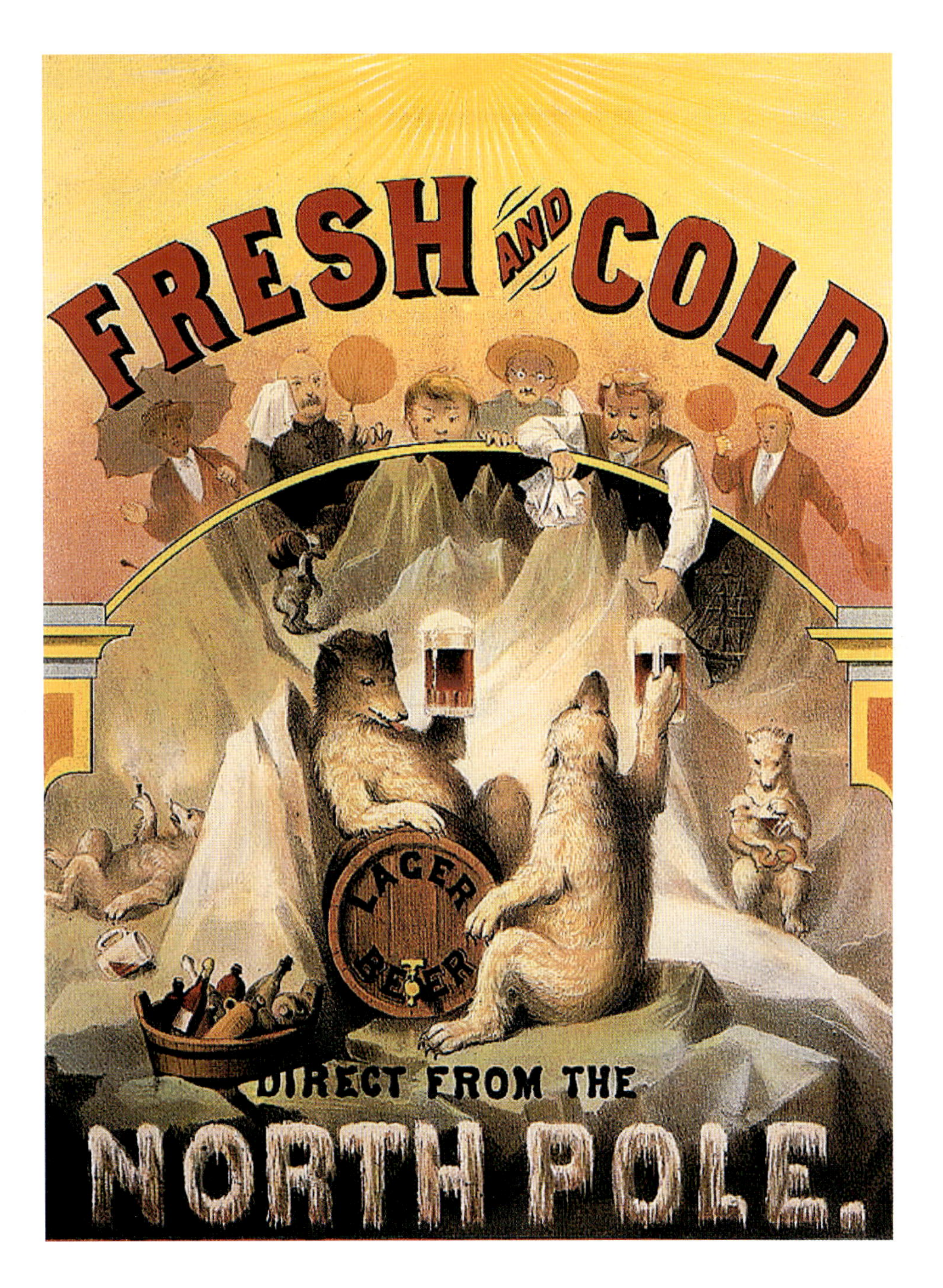

There's nothing better than a cold beer on a scorching summer day in Baltimore. This nineteenth-century advertising illustration is historically important in two ways. First, it shows that the "cold beer" paradigm is not new. Even back then, it was expected that lager would be served cold. Second, it shows that lager in the nineteenth century was a bold amber color, and not a withered, light yellow. Library of Congress via author's collection

In this building, Ulysses S. Grant and Robert E. Lee might *have—and perhaps* should *have—shared a round of beers in April 1865. They almost certainly did not, but when Lee surrendered to Grant in the McLean House at Appomattox, the Clover Hill Tavern (also known as the Patterson House) was just a few minutes ride away. Built in 1819, it is the oldest structure in the village of Appomattox Court House. The adjacent brewhouse, which also may have once housed slave quarters, is clearly visible in this photograph that was taken in the 1920s.* Library of Congress via author's collection

1849 Gold Rush. The precious yellow metal was discovered in phenomenal abundance in the Sierra Nevada foothills in 1848, and when the news reached the East, it touched off what has been characterized as the biggest voluntary mass migration in human history. San Francisco, a sleepy outpost on a perfect natural harbor, blossomed into a magnificent metropolis in less than two years. At the same time, the city of the Golden Gate became the most important brewing city west of the cities along the Mississippi River. It has been said that until the Civil War, half of all the United States breweries west of the Father of Waters were in San Francisco.

Hubert Howe Bancroft, who wrote the massive and definitive history of California's early days, notes that in 1837, a San Franciscan named William "Billy the Brewer" McGlove became the first Euro-American to brew beer west of the Mississippi, placing San Francisco before Milwaukee among America's great brewing cities. Other data indicates that bottled beer was being imported into San Francisco by 1843 and that ale and porter were abundantly available there by the Gold Rush year of 1849.

While San Francisco probably had many breweries by 1849, William Bull's Empire Brewery at Market and Second Streets is the earliest one mentioned in a city directory. Adam Schuppert's California Brewery is also noted in other sources as still being in existence in 1849. Though many breweries probably came and went

during these turbulent times, there were at least fifteen in San Francisco by 1856, including Schuppert's, Jacob Gundlach's Bavarian Brewery, Jacob Specht's San Francisco Brewery, and the Seidenstrecker & Rathe Washington Brewery. The Eagle and Eureka breweries were specifically listed brewers of ale and porter.

Brewing lager in San Francisco was problematic. As the Gold Rush swept California, the Lager Revolution swept the rest of the nation. It was only natural that the thirsty "Forty-Niners" would want a pint of lager. However, lager fermentation requires more than just lager yeast. It requires temperatures very near freezing. Like lager's native Bavaria, New York, Philadelphia, and Milwaukee take freezing temperatures for granted and early brewers could harvest enough ice in the winter for year-round storage.

While San Francisco's temperatures in the winter can dip below 32 degrees Fahrenheit with the wind-chill factor, it almost never actually freezes. In the 1850s, ice was imported from Alaska or brought down from the High Sierra by wagon. Both options were not economical for

Serving Belleville-brewed Stag Beer when it was photographed in July 1935, the Buck Tavern on Main Street in Columbia, Illinois, was built in about 1828. It was a popular stagecoach stop on the road south out of St. Louis, and it probably brewed on premises. A German named Grosse operated the tavern after 1860, and famous patrons ranging from Grover Cleveland to Mark Twain frequented the establishment. Library of Congress via author's collection

Right: *The drinking song* Wait for the Lager *was typical of popular music in the Lager Revolution era of the middle nineteenth century. A parody of* Wait for the Wagon, *it summarized the scene in a typical New York "bierkeller" with such words as "Where the Lager runs like blazes, and the music is so sweet/I'll order lots of liquor, and something nice to eat/We'll listen to the singers, they'll make you laugh and wink/So come into the cellar, and have a social drink."* Far right: *The nineteenth-century popular song* Lager Beer Jacob *was a parody on both the song* Champagne Charley *and on the accented English of first-generation German-Americans. Songs such as this mocked German speakers with such lyrics as "I goes out mit de Deutsches gals, in de gartens ve does shine/Und dere ve trinks our Lager-Beer, und juice from de dear Olt Rhine."* Library of Congress via author's collection

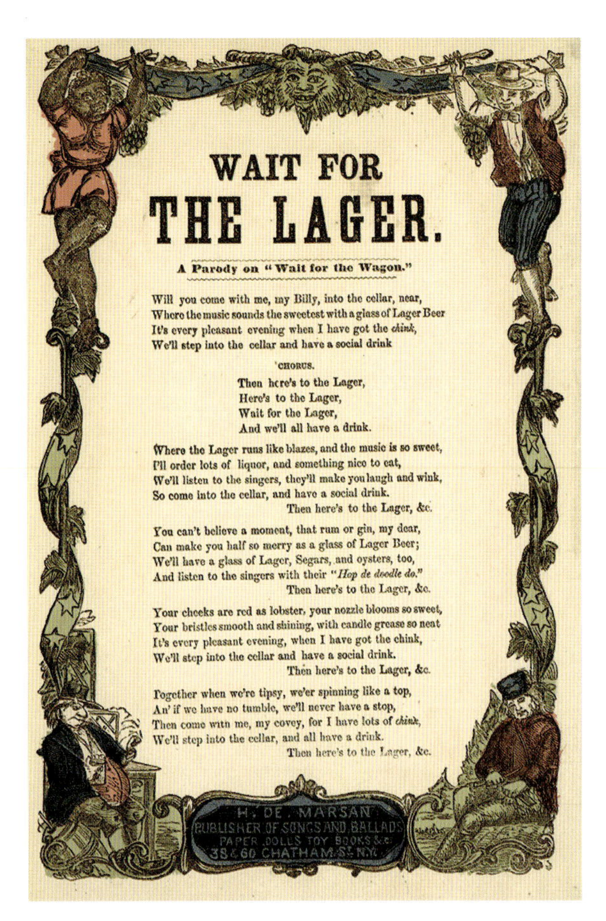

WAIT FOR THE LAGER.

A Parody on "Wait for the Wagon."

Will you come with me, my Billy, into the cellar, near,
Where the music sounds the sweetest with a glass of Lager Beer
It's every pleasant evening when I have got the *chink*,
We'll step into the cellar and have a social drink

CHORUS.

Then here's to the Lager,
Here's to the Lager,
Wait for the Lager,
And we'll all have a drink.

Where the Lager runs like blazes, and the music is so sweet,
I'll order lots of liquor, and something nice to eat,
We'll listen to the singers, they'll make you laugh and wink,
So come into the cellar, and have a social drink.
Then here's to the Lager, &c.

You can't believe a moment, that rum or gin, my dear,
Can make you half so merry as a glass of Lager Beer;
We'll have a glass of Lager, Segars, and oysters, too,
And listen to the singers with their "*Hop de doodle do.*"
Then here's to the Lager, &c.

Your cheeks are red as lobster, your nozzle blooms so sweet,
Your bristles smooth and shining, with candle grease so neat
It's every pleasant evening, when I have got the chink,
We'll step into the cellar and have a social drink.
Then here's to the Lager, &c.

Together when we're tipsy, we'er spinning like a top,
An' if we have no tumble, we'll never have a stop,
Then come with me, my covey, for I have lots of *chink*,
We'll step into the cellar, and all have a drink.
Then here's to the Lager, &c.

H. DE. MARSAN
PUBLISHER OF SONGS AND BALLADS
PAPER DOLLS TOY BOOKS &c
38 & 60 CHATHAM ST. N.Y.

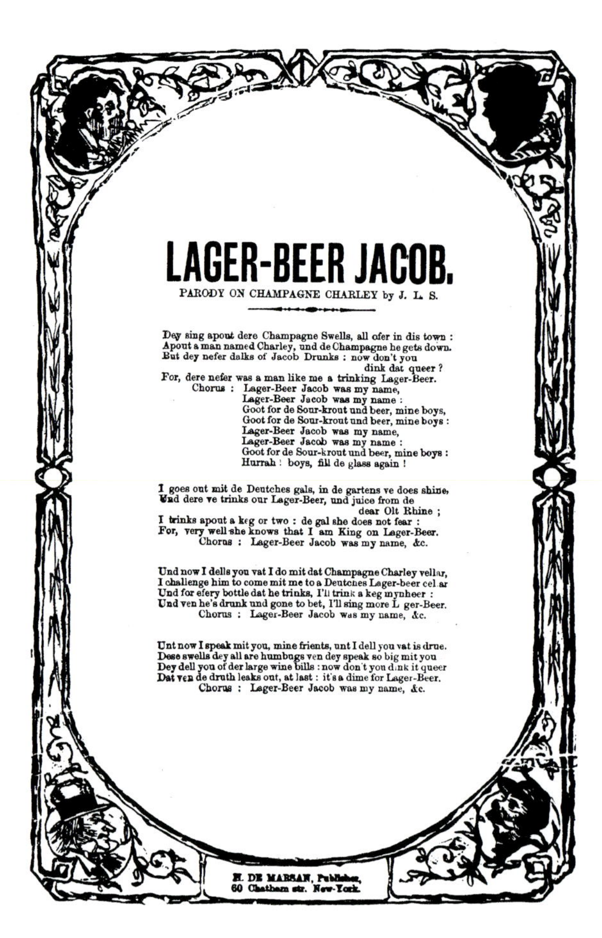

LAGER-BEER JACOB.

PARODY ON CHAMPAGNE CHARLEY by J. L. S.

Dey sing apout dere Champagne Swells, all ofer in dis town :
Apout a man named Charley, und de Champagne he gets down.
But dey nefer dalks of Jacob Drunks : now don't you dink dat queer ?
For, dere nefer was a man like me a trinking Lager-Beer.
Chorus : Lager-Beer Jacob was my name,
Lager-Beer Jacob was my name :
Goot for de Sour-krout und beer, mine boys,
Goot for de Sour-krout und beer, mine boys :
Lager-Beer Jacob was my name,
Lager-Beer Jacob was my name :
Goot for de Sour-krout und beer, mine boys :
Hurrah ! boys, fill de glass again !

I goes out mit de Deutches gals, in de gartens ve does shine,
Und dere ve trinks our Lager-Beer, und juice from de dear Olt Rhine ;
I trinks apout a keg or two : de gal she does not fear :
For, very well she knows that I am King on Lager-Beer.
Chorus : Lager-Beer Jacob was my name, &c.

Und now I dells you vat I do mit dat Champagne Charley vellar,
I challenge him to come mit me to a Deutches Lager-beer cellar
Und for efery bottle dat he trinks, I'll trink a keg mynheer :
Und ven he's drunk und gone to bet, I'll sing more Lager-Beer.
Chorus : Lager-Beer Jacob was my name, &c.

Unt now I speak mit you, mine frients, unt I dell you vat is drue.
Dese swells dey all are humbugs ven dey speak so big mit you
Dey dell you of der large wine bills : now don't you dink it queer
Dat ven de druth leaks out, at last : it's a dime for Lager-Beer.
Chorus : Lager-Beer Jacob was my name, &c.

H. DE MARSAN, Publisher,
60 Chatham str. New-York.

brewing. The solution, arrived at by an anonymous San Francisco brewer and soon adopted throughout the Golden State, was to ferment beer at warmer "ale" temperatures while using lager yeast. Because the yeast flourished as it continued to ferment at warmer than accustomed temperatures, there was a huge buildup of carbon dioxide and a large blast of foam and carbon dioxide when kegs were tapped. For this reason, this hybrid beer style was called "steam beer."

There were early breweries elsewhere in California, but nothing on the scale of what occurred in San Francisco. In the Sierra Nevada, breweries existed in gold-mining towns such as Placerville and Downieville in the 1850s. Christopher Kuhn is said to have established the first "lager" brewery in Los Angeles in 1854, but he probably was producing a product more like the San Franciscans' steam beer. Like San Francisco, The City of Angels was also at much of a loss for ice.

In the Pacific Northwest, the evolution of commercial brewing followed that of California—but not by much. In Oregon Territory, the new city of Portland—originally "Stumptown"—soon emerged as the brewing center of the Northwest. Coincidentally, it would take on a similar role 130 years later during the Microbrewery Revolution. The first brewery in Portland is believed to have been the City Brewery, established by Henry Saxer in 1852 and operated by him for exactly ten years. In 1862, he sold his brewery to Henry Weinhard, a man whose name would be closely associated with Oregon brewing for more than a century. Weinhard had come to Portland from just across the Columbia River in Vancouver, Washington. There, in 1859, he took over the brewery started by John (Johann) Muench in 1856. This was Washington's first commercial brewery.

During the last decade before the Civil War, there was an explosion in the volume of beer produced in the United States. From 431

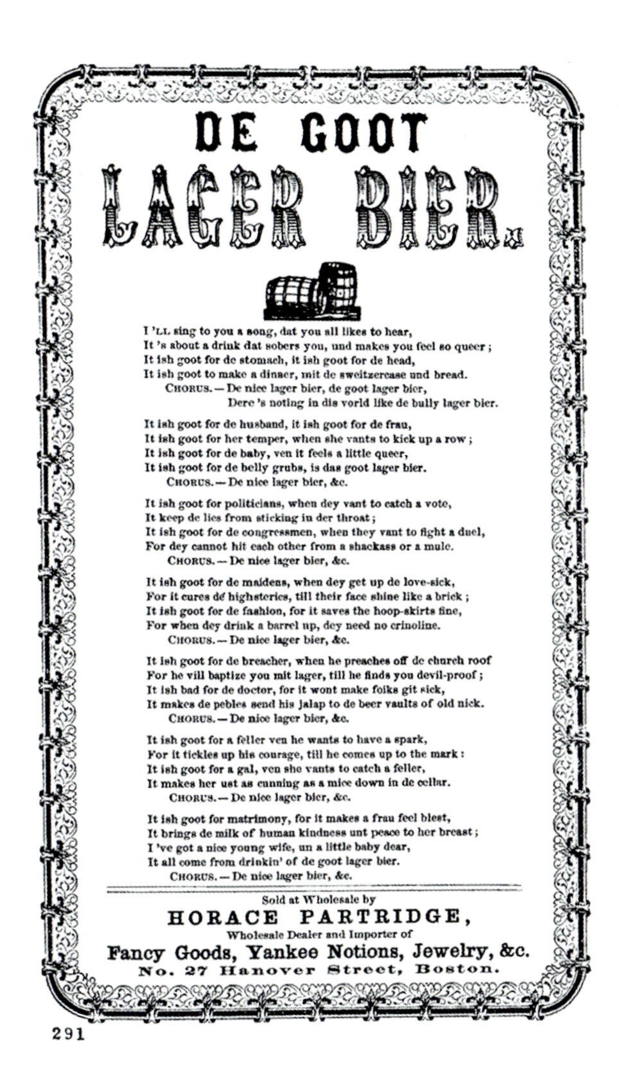

DE GOOT

LAGER BIER.

I 'LL sing to you a song, dat you all likes to hear,
It 's about a drink dat sobers you, und makes you feel so queer;
It ish goot for de stomach, it ish goot for de head,
It ish goot to make a dinner, mit de sweitzercase und bread.
CHORUS.—De nice lager bier, de goot lager bier,
Dere 's noting in dis vorld like de bully lager bier.

It ish goot for de husband, it ish goot for de frau,
It ish goot for her temper, when she vants to kick up a row;
It ish goot for de baby, ven it feels a little queer,
It ish goot for de belly grubs, is das goot lager bier.
CHORUS.—De nice lager bier, &c.

It ish goot for politicians, when dey vant to catch a vote,
It keep de lies from sticking in der throat;
It ish goot for de congressmen, when they vant to fight a duel,
For dey cannot hit each other from a shackass or a mule.
CHORUS.—De nice lager bier, &c.

It ish goot for de maidens, when dey get up de love-sick,
For it cures de highsterics, till their face shine like a brick;
It ish goot for de fashion, for it saves the hoop-skirts fine,
For when dey drink a barrel up, dey need no crinoline.
CHORUS.—De nice lager bier, &c.

It ish goot for de breacher, when he preaches off de church roof
For he vill baptize you mit lager, till he finds you devil-proof;
It ish bad for de doctor, for it wont make folks git sick,
It makes de pebles send his jalap to de beer vaults of old nick.
CHORUS.—De nice lager bier, &c.

It ish goot for a feller ven he wants to have a spark,
For it tickles up his courage, till he comes up to the mark:
It ish goot for a gal, ven she vants to catch a feller,
It makes her ust as cunning as a mice down in de cellar.
CHORUS.—De nice lager bier, &c.

It ish goot for matrimony, for it makes a frau feel blest,
It brings de milk of human kindness unt peace to her breast;
I 've got a nice young wife, un a little baby dear,
It all come from drinkin' of de goot lager bier.
CHORUS.—De nice lager bier, &c.

Sold at Wholesale by
HORACE PARTRIDGE,
Wholesale Dealer and Importer of
Fancy Goods, Yankee Notions, Jewelry, &c.
No. 27 Hanover Street, Boston.

291

Making fun of German accents was popular grist for songwriters of the middle nineteenth century. Beer, especially lager, was almost always mentioned. In Goot Lager Bier, *the moral of the story is summarized with "It is goot for matrimony, for it makes a frau feel blest/It brings de milk of human kindness und peace to her breast/I've got a nice young wife, und a little baby dear/It all come from drinkin' of de goot lager bier."* Library of Congress via author's collection

American breweries in 1850, the number nearly tripled to 1,269 in 1860. Most of these were lager breweries. Indeed, the number of ale and porter breweries in 1860 was probably less than in 1850. More than three-quarters of the production was still centered in New York and Pennsylvania, but the fastest-growing centers were in the upper Midwest, especially in Chicago and Milwaukee.

Farther west, the handful of breweries between the Mississippi and the Pacific that were born between the Gold Rush and the Civil War were just a harbinger of what was to come after the war.

During the Civil War, the brewing industry, which was primarily concentrated north of the Mason-Dixon Line, supported the Union war effort in unexpected ways. In 1861, the Internal Revenue System was established to use income taxes to finance the war. The following year, the brewing industry was singled out and a one-dollar tax was levied on each barrel of beer produced in the United States. In response to government taxation and a growing temperance movement, 37 breweries in New York City came together in 1862 to form the industry's first trade organization, which became known as the United States Brewers' Association in 1864. This organization would grow and expand with the industry for the next half-century.

The end of the war would bring a number of social and economic changes. For the brewing industry, it would be a Golden Age of American brewing, marked by two important trends: the evolution of the giant megabrewers and the proliferation of hometown breweries throughout the United States. While these trends seem to be—and were—contradictory, they would exist in harmony during the Golden Age, and would not cross one another until the next century.

1892
BREW ★ HOUSE
RAILROAD DEPOT
PESTALOZZI ST.
NO PARKING
THIS SIDE
ANY TIME

Chapter 4: The Rise of the Great Dynasties 1865-1920

The United States was in an expansive mood after the Civil War. The railroad network in the Northeast and the Plains states had grown during the war, and the long-anticipated Transcontinental Railroad—built and operated jointly by the Central Pacific and Union Pacific—linked California to the rest of the nation in 1869. The economy continued to expand and, along with it, so did the demand for beer.

The number of breweries in the United States continued to mushroom. As noted in Chapter 3, that number tripled between 1850 and 1860. By 1873, it had more than tripled again—from 1,269 to 4,131. Also significant was the increased production. From just over a million barrels in 1860, output grew to *nine* million barrels annually. This meant that the breweries averaged about 800 barrels per year in 1860, and close to 2,200 barrels per year by 1873.

However, the word "average" is misleading. There was no such thing as an average brewery. Although the majority of breweries were still small-scale operations, certain companies began to emerge as industrial giants.

Because of its size, New York City remained an important brewing center after the Civil War, but Milwaukee would soon eclipse it. At the time when George Ehret in New York City (see Chapter 5) had the largest brewery in the country, those on the tier just below him were located in Milwaukee, despite the fact that the city had a tiny fraction of New York City's population. Not only had the Milwaukee brewers learned the importance of wider distribution, the Great Chicago Fire of 1871 destroyed or crippled many Chicago breweries and caused the Windy City's thirsty citizens to turn to the products of nearby Milwaukee.

Opposite: *The grand Anheuser-Busch Brewery building in St.Louis, Missouri, as photographed by Alexander Piaget in about 1937. Built in 1892 in the style of all the great nineteenth-century brewery buildings, it was designed by the firm of Widman, Walsh & Boisselier of St. Louis.* Library of Congress via author's collection. Inset: *The famous "A-&-Eagle" insignia sits prominently on the Anheuser-Busch St. Louis brewery building. Eberhard Anheuser first used the logo on packaging in 1872. Since then, it has evolved into one of the longest-lived and most widely seen brewery trademarks in the world.* Bill Yenne

Below: *The big stone eagle stands watch over the massive Anheuser-Busch brewery building in St. Louis on a cold, clear winter morning. The building was completed in 1892 under the hands-on direction of Adolphus Busch himself, and it is the centerpiece of the greatest brewing empire in history.* Bill Yenne

Above: *Adolphus Busch used advanced ice-making technology and a company-owned railroad to turn his father-in-law's St. Louis brewery into a major Midwest institution. He died in 1913, after founding the brewing dynasty that would later turn Anheuser-Busch into the biggest brewing company in the world.* Author illustration

Meanwhile, a general momentum gathered toward consolidation. After the "Panic" (Recession) of 1873, numerous marginal, smaller breweries closed. As the number of breweries declined from their all-time high of 4,131, demand continued to increase with the overall population. The Milwaukee brewers had the momentum, the desire, and capability for expansion.

The great dynasties that produced Milwaukee's famous beers included those of the Best brothers, Frederick Miller, Captain Frederick Pabst, Valentin Blatz, and Joseph Schlitz. It was the Schlitz company that coined the advertising slogan, "The Beer That Made Milwaukee Famous." The implication was that Milwaukee *was* famous *because* of its beer.

As indicated in Chapter 3, the Best family constituted Milwaukee's original brewing dynasty.

Left: *A uniformed driver and a team of Clydesdales prepare for a delivery run from the Anheuser-Busch flagship brewery in St. Louis. The Clydesdale teams remain to this day as one of the best-loved Anheuser-Busch trademarks.* San Francisco History Center via author's collection

Jacob Best started his Empire Brewery in 1844 and it was there that his four sons—Charles, Lorenz, Philip, and Jacob Jr.—would learn the brewer's trade. In 1850, Charles left to start the Plank Road Brewery in nearby Wauwatosa. Lorenz joined him in 1851, but two years later they sold the brewery to Frederick Miller.

Meanwhile, Philip and Jacob Jr. remained with their father, taking over the management of the Empire Brewery in 1853. In 1860, when Philip became the sole owner, the company became the Philip Best Company. By that time, Philip's daughters had both married young men who were interested in the brewing industry—Emil Schandien and Captain Frederick Pabst.

Philip Best retired in 1864 and placed his two sons-in-law in charge of the company that he'd inherited from his father. The corporate family tree that began two decades earlier with Jacob Best Sr. included three of the principal names in Milwaukee brewing history—Best, Miller, and Pabst. Schandien would soon be eclipsed by his ambitious brother-in-law.

By the 1870s, with Pabst's hand at the throttle, the Philip Best Company had become the largest brewery in Milwaukee, and was second only to George Ehret's huge New York City company nationally.

Captain Pabst would not remain second for long. He took sole control of the company in 1889, and renamed it Pabst Brewing. Four years later, it was America's largest brewery and also the first in the United States to exceed one million barrels of production annually. Pabst cast his distribution network far and wide, from the farms and cities of the upper Midwest to the sparsely populated plains and Mountain West. In 1899, he audaciously began exporting into New York City, where the local brewers had a volume unmatched nearly everywhere but in Milwaukee. He even opened a Pabst Hotel in New York. The captain

A group of young folks greet two horses pulling an Anheuser-Busch brewery wagon in Charlotte, North Carolina. Because there were not any operating breweries in North Carolina during the late nineteenth and early twentieth centuries, the state was prime marketing territory for megabrewers like Anheuser-Busch. Library of Congress via author's collection

certainly had a flair for the dramatic. He introduced the practice of tying blue ribbons around the necks of his bottles, thus launching the immortal brand, Pabst Blue Ribbon.

Pabst certainly overshadowed Frederick Miller, whose Miller Brewing Company occupied the other limb of the Jacob Best Sr. corporate family tree. Nevertheless, Miller's company remained an important factor and one of the leading brewers in Milwaukee for the next century. From tenth place nationally and third in Milwaukee, Miller would emerge in the late 1970s as the second largest brewing company in the United States after Anheuser-Busch.

Frederick Miller passed away in 1888 and was succeeded by two of his sons. Ernest remained active in company affairs until 1922, and Frederick A. Miller stayed involved until 1947.

With Miller Brewing perpetually in third place locally, Pabst's biggest Milwaukee rival was Joseph Schlitz. Despite Schlitz's slogan, Pabst always figured that *he,* not Schlitz, had made Milwaukee famous.

Joseph (Josef) Schlitz was born in Mainz in the German state of Hesse and came to Milwaukee in 1850 at the age of 20. He then went to work for August Krug, a recent German immigrant who had started his own brewery in 1849 on Chestnut Street, across from David Gipfel's pioneer lager brewery. When Krug died in 1856, Schlitz took over management of the company. Two years later, Schlitz married Anna Krug, August's widow, and he renamed the company Joseph Schlitz Brewing.

The Great Chicago Fire of 1871 helped propel Schlitz to the forefront of Milwaukee brewing when he led the effort to get emergency supplies of beer into the decimated city. Though other Milwaukee brewers became involved in this essential relief effort, the people of Chicago saw and remembered the Schlitz brand name. It was a charitable act that turned into a public relations coup. If Schlitz made Milwaukee famous, it was the 1871 fire that made *his* name famous. Within a few years, Schlitz emerged from the pack to become Milwaukee's number two brewer behind Captain Pabst.

In 1875, Joseph Schlitz decided to make a trip back to Germany to visit relatives. But the successful businessman cousin from America never arrived in Mainz. The steamship on which he was traveling ran aground off Britain and Schlitz drowned. Widowed a second time, Anna lived until 1887.

With Schlitz's death, control of Joseph Schlitz Brewing passed to August Uilein and his brothers.

Opposite: *A massive row of gleaming copper beer kettles at the Pabst brewery in Milwaukee boldly projected the power of the brewery that was America's largest in the 1890s. The kettles were called "dreadnoughts" because they reminded people of battleships.* Milwaukee County Historical Society via author's collection

Top left: *Joseph Schlitz brewed "The Beer That Made Milwaukee Famous." He arrived in the Wisconsin city from Mainz, Germany, went to work as a brewer, and eventually became one of the leading figures in Milwaukee at a time when it was the brewing capital of North America.* Author illustration

Below: *The Joseph Schlitz Brewing Company positioned its product as the beer that defined the brewing capital of America. Schlitz was, they said, the "Beer That Made Milwaukee Famous." Schlitz himself died in 1875, and it was under his successor, August Uilein, that the company officially adopted the slogan in 1893.* Author's collection

Above: *The Stecher Cooperage Works produced containers—primarily of reinforced oak—for the beverage industry. Because of the company's location in St. Louis, it probably sold a lot more beer kegs than wine casks. This ad appeared in 1905.* Author's collection

Right: *Valentin "Val" Blatz started his Milwaukee brewery in 1851, right next door to Johann Braun's City Brewery. A year later, he married Braun's widow and merged the two firms. Blatz died in 1894, after building the company into one of the city's most important brewers.* Author illustration

The Krug family had befriended August Uilein when he was a child, and Schlitz had hired the 16-year-old Uilein as a bookkeeper in 1858. Uilein had worked in St. Louis from 1860 to 1868, but he returned to the Schlitz company and worked his way up the corporate ladder. He would manage the company for 36 years (even longer than Schlitz) until his death in 1911.

During Uilein's tenure, Schlitz Brewing solidified its position as the number two brewer in Milwaukee and in the top five nationally. In 1879, Schlitz produced 110,832 barrels to Pabst's 180,152. In 1893, it was August Uilein who formally adopted the slogan "The Beer That Made Milwaukee Famous."

Valentin "Val" Blatz was a Milwaukee brewing legend who was always overshadowed by the city's

two megabrewers. Nevertheless, he played an important part in shaping the city's mystique. His company would become Milwaukee's number three brewery for much of the latter part of the nineteenth century. Born in Germany in 1826, Blatz arrived in Milwaukee around 1850 and started his brewery next door to Johann Braun's City Brewery. When Braun died in 1852, Blatz married Braun's widow and consolidated the two firms as the Val Blatz Brewery.

In 1889, a consortium of British financiers, doing business as Milwaukee & Chicago Breweries Ltd., proposed a takeover and consolidation of Milwaukee's big three. Pabst and Schlitz laughed off the scheme, but Blatz parted with a share in his company.

In 1858, across the state of Wisconsin in LaCrosse, John Gund and Gottlieb Heileman founded their small City Brewery on South Third Street. Gund, who had previously owned another company in LaCrosse, left Heileman in 1872 and went independent again. Gottlieb Heileman continued to build his business, as did his family after his death in 1878. The G. Heileman Brewing Company would eventually grow to national prominence, not through the vehicle of a single national brand like Pabst or Schlitz, but through an amazing amalgam of important, formerly independent brands, including—nearly a century later—Blatz.

Jacob Leinenkugel Brewing Company of Chippewa Falls is an example of another small-town Wisconsin brewing company that was born in the years after the Civil War and is still a household name today. It was founded in 1867 by its namesake and John Miller, who was Leinenkugel's partner for the next sixteen years. Located atop Big Eddy Springs, the brewery operated as Spring Brewery until 1898 and has long been known for its distinctive "Indian maiden head" logo. The logo reflects the brewery's location in "Indian Head Country," which refers to the profile created on maps by the meandering St. Croix River along the Wisconsin–Minnesota border near Chippewa Falls. The brand survived through most of the twentieth century as a strong

During the late nineteenth century, Pabst Brewing marketed not only beer, but also Malt Extract product to provide consumers with "vim and bounce." Presumably, the beer also imparted these qualities. As evident from the glazed expression on this wide-eyed young lady, Pabst Malt Extract was certainly "vivifying." Author's collection

Frederick Pabst was a Great Lakes steamship captain who married the daughter of Milwaukee brewery owner Philip Best. He ended up "captain" of the company, which he built into Milwaukee's largest. He had a flair for promotion and saw his blue-ribboned beer bottles distributed from the Dakotas to New York City. Author illustration

independent with a very devoted following. In 1987, Miller Brewing of Milwaukee purchased the company, but it remained an autonomous operating unit and entered the twenty-first century as one of the top dozen breweries in the United States.

Even as a major brewing center in the years after the Civil War, St. Louis, Missouri, was eclipsed in importance by Milwaukee, Philadelphia, New York, Chicago, and even San Francisco. However, the huge brewery that developed from the little firm started on Carondelet Avenue in 1852 by George Schneider has forever earned St. Louis a preeminent place in the pages of American brewing history.

In 1857 Schneider, like so many small brewers throughout history, realized that he could no longer compete with bigger companies. He sold his little Bavarian Brewery to Adam and Phillip Carl Hammer, who were underwritten by a loan from a wealthy St. Louis soap maker named Eberhard Anheuser. In 1860, when the brewery once again verged on collapse, Anheuser realized he needed to take direct control of operations in order to protect his investment. The firm became known as E. Anheuser & Company's Bavarian Brewery.

Within a year after Anheuser entered the brewing business, his daughter Lily Anheuser married a 22-year-old brewery supply salesman named Adolphus Busch. In 1864, Busch joined his father-in-law's firm as a salesman. Five years later, he became a partner. In 1875 the Bavarian Brewery name was dropped and the brewery became E. Anheuser and Company's Brewing Association. In 1879, it became the Anheuser-Busch Brewing Association. The following year, upon the death of Eberhard Anheuser, Busch became the president.

Busch soon proved himself as one of American brewing's first great marketing geniuses. He was not the first to dream of an American national beer—indeed, Captain Pabst had already perfected interstate marketing—but he was the first to truly realize the dream.

St. Louis was a mid-sized town with a fairly good market for beer, but nothing compared to Milwaukee or New York. Some men would have been content to be the part owner of a successful, medium-sized brewery in St. Louis, but not Adolphus Busch. Even before becoming president, he launched a vigorous advertising campaign and formed a wide distribution network. He established a network of icehouses on railroad sidings to keep long-distance shipments of beer cool and fresh. He was the first to vigorously promote the new technology of artificial ice making, and in 1877 he became the first brewer to ship his beer in refrigerated railcars. Later, he helped pioneer the pasteurization of beer.

Busch dreamed of a national beer, a brew specially designed to appeal to people of all walks of life throughout the United States. Along with his friend Carl Conrad, Busch created such a beer (a lager, of course), which was introduced in 1876, the centennial of United States independence.

Busch and Conrad considered the recipe and the name of their "people's beer" carefully. The most popular brews of the day were lagers brewed in the manner of central Europe's golden triangle (Bavaria–Austria–Bohemia), and many breweries produced brand names that alluded to that region. Indeed, the Anheuser-Busch Brewery had started as George Schneider's Bavarian Brewery, but it was merely one of many breweries that used the name "Bavarian." Of the golden lagers, the pale ones from the Bohemian corner of the triangle, the pilsners, epitomized the style Busch and Conrad wanted.

According to Gerald Holland, writing in the October 1929 issue of *The American Mercury*, Conrad traveled to Europe and found the specific recipe in a specific Bohemian brewing city known in the Czech language as Ceske Budejovice. Since the city was then part of the Austro-Hungarian Empire, it was better known by its German name,

A nineteenth-century workman thoughtfully pauses to enjoy a stein of beer and a smoke. It was common during the era for workmen to carry their own steins to the job site. At break time, beer was brought from the local brewery in a bucket by one of the youngsters who invariably congregated around job sites. The familiar call was "Send the boy for a bucket of beer!" Author's collection

This belt-driven keg scrubber is typical of those that were used at all major breweries during the late nineteenth century. Scalding water was used to clean the kegs, but never soap because it damaged the beer and contaminated the kegs. Author illustration

Budweis. In the nineteenth century, as in the twenty-first century, the Budweis brewery brewed a beer that was called "Budweiser," just as beer brewed in Bavaria was called "Bavarian," beer from Prague was called "Prager," and beer from Pilsen was (and is) called "pilsner."

Adolphus Busch may or may not have had the Czech-speaking Bohemian town in mind when he chose "Budweiser" as the appellation of the beer that he planned to be his flagship brand. According to an Associated Press article appearing in the February 28, 2000, issue of *Modern Brewery Age* magazine, "Anheuser-Busch claims that it registered the Budweiser trademark in the United States in 1878, nineteen years before the Czech brewery formally adopted the same name."

According to an 1894 letter from Adolphus Busch to trademark attorney Rowland Cox, he selected the Budweiser name "because it was easily pronounceable by Americans and was not the name of any beer then sold in America."

Budweiser has not only survived as a brand name, it has prospered. By the latter part of the twentieth century, it had become the biggest-selling single brand in the United States and in the world, just as Anheuser-Busch had become the world's biggest brewing company.

ADOLPH COORS
C
TRADE MARK
GOLDEN, COLORADO.
Adolph Coors' GOLDEN BREWERY
Adolph Coors' GOLDEN BREWERY

Chapter 5: The Rise of the Great Regionals 1865-1920

The post–Civil War momentum toward consolidation, which laid the foundation for the national breweries, also benefited the rise of the great regionals. In the late nineteenth century, Schlitz, Pabst, and Anheuser-Busch were still essentially regionals, albeit within large and growing regions. While Milwaukee was emerging as the brewing capital of America, and its brewers became the royal families of American brewing, there were other great names, such as Bernard Stroh in Detroit. In Minnesota, there were men like Jacob Schmidt and the legendary Theodore Hamm. In San Francisco, there were Charles Hansen and John Wieland. Portland had Henry Weinhard, and in Colorado, there was a man named Adolph Coors.

New York City, which lay at the center of North America's largest metropolitan area, experienced the rise of a number of major brewing companies. The difference between New York City and Milwaukee—or between New York City and *anywhere*—was the sheer size of the market. A brewery in Manhattan or Brooklyn had a market within a half-day's drive of a beer wagon that was much greater than the markets in Milwaukee and Chicago combined. While the Milwaukee brewers thought outside of the box—or outside of state lines—their New York City counterparts didn't have to.

The biggest brewery in the United States during the decade after the Civil War was that of George Ehret. Trained as a brewer in Germany, Ehret had arrived in New York City in 1857 at the age of 22. Ehret is said to have gone to work for Anton Hupfel, whose brewery was located at Third Avenue and 161st Street.

Opposite: *This excellent color view shows the Adolph Coors Golden Brewery in Golden, Colorado, as it appeared late in the nineteenth century. Coors and his partner, Jacob Schueler, situated their original brewery on this site in 1873 in order to take advantage of the available spring water. The inset shows the company's shipping depot in nearby Denver.* Coors via author's collection

The main building of the Germania Brewery in Allentown, Pennsylvania, was completed in April 1913, replacing the original Germania Brewery that was built on South Seventh Street in 1878 by Benedict Nuding. The "new" brewery operated until 1967, primarily under the Neuweiler name, and closed just before this photograph was taken. Library of Congress via author's collection

In 1866, Ehret struck out on his own, building his own lager brewery on 92nd Street between Second and Third Avenues in the Yorkville district of New York City. The location was auspicious, for nearby 86th Street would be the nexus of German-American culture for the next century.

As for the name of his new enterprise, Ehret borrowed the centuries-old appellation of a treacherous section of the nearby East River. George Ehret's Hell Gate Brewery produced its first brew in January 1867, and within five years it was producing nearly 34,000 barrels annually. Production topped 100,000 barrels in 1874 and exceeded 180,000 within five years, making Hell Gate the largest brewery on the continent. The brewery's physical plant grew to encompass an entire city block, with stables and other facilities reaching as far north as 94th Street. The company surpassed 400,000 barrels in 1890 and would exceed 600,000 annually by the turn of the century.

Ballantine was another great name in the history of New York City brewing. In the New York City metropolitan area, Ballantine was one of the last great English names in nineteenth century American brewing. In 1833, Peter Ballantine set up shop in Albany, but moved his operation to Newark, New Jersey, in 1840. At that point, he joined forces with Erastus Patterson to acquire a brewery that had been founded by General John Cumming in 1805. Peter Ballantine became the sole proprietor of the company in 1847.

By 1879, P. Ballantine & Sons was the second largest brewing operation in the New York City area, with an annual output of more than 100,000 barrels. In that same year, the company acquired a second brewery in Newark from the Schalk Brothers, who had begun brewing in 1852.

A third brand name destined to become a household word in New York City during the half-century following the Civil War was Schaefer. Frederick Schaefer arrived in New York City from Prussia in 1838, and went to work brewing beer for Sebastian Sommers's new brewery on Broadway near 18th Street. A couple of years later, when lager suddenly came on the scene in Germany, there were excited ripples throughout the German-American community. At about this time, Frederick's brother, Maximilian, arrived in New York City with a sample of lager yeast. In 1842, Frederick Schaefer bought out his boss and he and Max began brewing lager.

After briefly occupying the Sommers brewery site, the brothers moved to Seventh Avenue near West 16th Street in 1845, and to Fourth Avenue (later Park Avenue) and East 51st Street, just north of where the New York Central Railroad would later build Grand Central Station. Frederick died in 1897, and Max passed away in 1904. By that time, the F. & M. Schaefer Brewing Company had grown into one of New York's great brewing enterprises. Max's son and heir, Rudolf Schaefer, bought out Frederick's heirs and took sole control of the company.

In 1916, after 67 years in their huge, redbrick landmark brewery on Park Avenue, Rudolf

A copper beer bottle frieze on the bottling house canopy at the Germania/Neuweiler Brewery. The original bottle line had opened in 1906 and was then capable of packaging 100 barrels per day. This plant opened on the eve of Prohibition and was largely idle for over a decade. Library of Congress via author's collection

The magnificent Tivoli-Union Brewery building in Denver, Colorado, was constructed in about 1895. Originally known as the Milwaukee Brewery, it was renamed in 1900 when John Good acquired it. It became the Tivoli-Union in 1934 after Prohibition, but the "Union" suffix was dropped in 1953. The brewery remained in Good's family until 1964. The following year it was sold to Carl and Joseph Occhiato, and its brewing ceased in 1969. Library of Congress via author's collection

Above: *Bernard (Bernhardt) Stroh arrived in Detroit from Germany by way of Brazil in 1849. A year later he began his own brewery, which became known as the Lion Brewery, after the Civil War. When Bernard died in 1882, his son renamed the company after the family. By the turn of the century, Stroh had evolved into the largest brewery in Detroit.* Author illustration

Schaefer became one of the first big Manhattan brewers to move all operations to Brooklyn. He selected a vast tract on Kent Street overlooking the East River. Unfortunately, construction on the new plant coincided with the gathering darkness of the impending Prohibition.

In Detroit, the name that would emerge as the dominant regional brand was Stroh. Bernard (Bernhardt) Stroh started his brewery on Catherine Street in 1850, but moved it twice, first to Gratiot Avenue and later to Elizabeth Street. Between 1864 and 1882, the company was known as the Lion Brewery after the heraldic insignia that had always been part of the company logo and bottle labels. The Stroh name was re-adopted in

1882 and retained until the company folded in 1999. Throughout the latter nineteenth century and through most of the twentieth, Stroh was Detroit's largest brewing company. In the 1980s, after acquiring Schlitz, Stroh became one of the top four brewing companies in the United States.

In Cincinnati, the large German population supported a number of sizable breweries. By the 1890s, per capita beer consumption in Cincinnati was greater than in any other major United States city. Among the breweries satiating this thirst was that of Christian Moerlein. Started in 1853, it was the eighth largest nationally by 1879. Another important Cincinnati regional was the Buckeye (originally Buckeye Street) Brewery, founded on Buckeye Street in 1852 and acquired by Ludwig Hudepohl and George Kotte in 1885. The latter died in 1893, and Ludwig "Louis" Hudepohl II bought out his widow in 1900. Thereafter, Hudepohl Brewing emerged as a Cincinnati landmark. Unlike Moerlein, it survived Prohibition and flourished in mid-century.

In the Twin Cities of Minneapolis and St. Paul, an inter-city rivalry defined the region's taste for beer for more than a century. Minneapolis Brewing & Malting originated in 1890 through a merger of the city's four largest brewing companies. Foremost among these was the brewery founded by John Orth in 1850. The others were Heinrich Brewing, dating back to 1866; Zahler & Noerenberg Brewing, founded by Anton Zahler in 1870; and Germania Brewing, started in 1884. The huge brewery erected in 1892 on the site of Orth's brewery would become famous throughout the upper Midwest for its Grain Belt brand.

Meanwhile, across the Mississippi River in St. Paul, a German immigrant named Theodore Hamm acquired a four-year-old brewery started by Andrew Keller in 1860. By 1886, when William Hamm joined his father's company, it was the second largest brewing operation in Minnesota. However, like Grain Belt, the Hamm name had become well known beyond the state.

In the years after the Civil War, the South was a long time in rebuilding its industrial infrastructure.

Above: *The Tivoli Beer wall sign, the smokestack, the Tivoli-Union tower, and the adjacent West Denver Turnhalle are pictured. The Turnhalle was a large, German-American community center completed in 1882. Naturally, it was adjacent to the brewery. A shallow three-story connector was constructed in 1890 to unite the two buildings.* Library of Congress via author's collection

Left: *Theodore Hamm acquired Andrew Keller's Pittsburgh Brewery in St. Paul, Minnesota, in 1864. He then renamed it after himself and built it into one of the most powerful breweries in Minnesota.* Author illustration

The top of the tower at the Tivoli-Union. Malted grain was gravity-fed from here to a grinder that was manufactured in the nineteenth century by the Seck Brothers of Dresden, Germany. Library of Congress via author's collection

Peter Schoenhofen and Matthias Gottfried started their brewing company in Chicago in 1858 (some sources say 1860), and moved to this site on Canalport Avenue in about 1864. Peter became the sole owner of the Schoenhofen Brewing Company in 1867, which merged into the National Brewing conglomerate in 1879. This magnificent building was constructed as the National-owned Schoenhofen Brewery in 1902. Library of Congress via author's collection

In the case of the brewing industry, the region was largely devoid of major industrial-strength breweries until after World War II. No region of the country has had fewer breweries in its history, and one southern state, Mississippi, didn't claim a commercial brewery until the era of the Milwaukee revolution.

An exception in the South was the city of New Orleans. Three brewpub owners who had been doing business in the 1850s—Joseph Christen, L. Fasnacht, and George Mertz—reopened after the Civil War and were joined by eight others within five years. Big breweries on the scale of those that existed in the North appeared in New Orleans around the turn of the century, including the Jackson Brewery on Decatur Street in the French Quarter, opened in 1890, and the Dixie Brewery, which opened on Tulane Street in 1907. The Jackson Brewery—and its signature brand, Jax Beer—survived until 1974, but the Dixie Brewing Company is still extant in the twenty-first century.

Texas, especially San Antonio, experienced a greater influx of German immigrants than anywhere else south of the Mason-Dixon Line, and a half-dozen breweries were operating in the area in the decades following the Civil War. Two of the most important breweries were the one started on the north side of town by J.B. Behloradsky in 1881, and the Lone Star Brewery, started on the south side in 1884 by Adolphus Busch. Though Busch also owned Anheuser-Busch, Lone Star was separately held. The brewery closed with Prohibition, although the name was revived at a new site in the 1930s. Behloradsky's brewery, known simply as San Antonio Brewing after 1883, began using the Pearl Beer brand name in 1886, and officially became Pearl Brewing in 1952.

Another important Texas regional was the Spoetzl Brewery in the town of Shiner, located about an hour east of San Antonio. This company evolved from the Shiner Brewing Association that was started in 1909, when it was taken over by the Betzold and Spoetzl partnership in 1915. It would survive Prohibition and end the twentieth century as the oldest surviving Texas independent.

In the Mountain West, two major regional brewing centers emerged in the latter half of the nineteenth century—Denver in Colorado Territory and the Anaconda-Butte-Helena triangle in Montana Territory. These areas also emerged as major mining centers for gold and other precious metals at the same time.

Denver's first brewery, the Rocky Mountain Brewery on Cherry Creek, was taken over by early Colorado pioneer John Good in 1861, two years after it was started. A master brewer from Europe, Good had arrived in 1859 with one of the first wagon trains bound for Denver. After a year of partnership with Philip Zang, Good moved on and the company became Philip Zang Brewing, which flourished until Prohibition.

Good's next move was to Aspen, where he operated in an off-and-on partnership with Jacob Mack through the 1880s and 1890s. In 1900, Good took control of a Denver brewery called the Milwaukee Brewery, which had been founded in 1864 and operated since 1879 by Max Melsheimer and John Mack. Good renamed the enterprise the Tivoli Brewery, after Tivoli Gardens in Copenhagen. Known as the Western Products Company during Prohibition, it reemerged as Tivoli-Union in 1934. The "Union" suffix was dropped in 1953, and for six years beginning in 1958, it was also known as the Mountain Brewing Company. The company remained under the ownership of the Good family and their descendants until 1965.

In the foothills of the Rockies, about a half-day's ride from Denver, the town of Golden, Colorado, got its first brewery, the Golden City, in 1868, but it folded in 1874. In the meantime, Jacob Schueler and Adolph Coors started Golden's second brewing company, the Golden Brewery, in 1873. Adolph Coors had apprenticed for several breweries in Germany before immigrating to the United States in 1868 at the age of 21. After a stint at the Stenger Brewery in Naperville, Illinois, he headed west to Colorado.

The Dixie Brewery on Tulane Street in New Orleans was one of the greatest classic brewery buildings ever built in the South. Completed in 1907, it reigned supreme until the consolidation period of the 1970s. Bill Yenne

A sign on Butte's Lincoln Hotel still proudly proclaims that Butte Special is "Montana's Finest Beer." Butte Brewing evolved from the brewery originally started in 1885 by Henry Muntzler, the "godfather" of Butte brewmasters. The company was the only one of the three Butte breweries extant in 1918 to reopen after Prohibition. It survived until 1963, when the mining industry went south—literally. (Chilean copper replaced Montana copper on the world market.) Bill Yenne

Coors and Schueler did not become successful in the gold fields by mining, but by providing the gold miners with golden lager. Coors bought out his partner in 1880. By 1890, Coors Brewing & Malting was producing 17,600 barrels annually, a fivefold increase over its 1880 output.

Thomas Smith started Montana's first brewery at Virginia City in 1863, one year before Montana became a territory with Virginia City as its capital. In 1874, Helena replaced Virginia City as the territorial capital and in 1883, the Northern Pacific Railroad linked Montana's rich mining towns with the outside world. One of the state's most famous breweries was founded in Helena by Charles Beehrer in 1864, and taken over two years later by Nicholas Kessler, an immigrant from Luxembourg. In 1886, Kessler built a new brewery on the site, which included the first refrigeration unit ever used in Montana and the first carbonic acid machine installed in a United States brewery. Kessler died in 1901, but the brewery operated until 1958. In 1982, the Kessler brand was revived in Helena by a microbrewery known as Montana Beverages.

While Kessler may have been a leading name in nineteenth-century Montana brewing, another man worth a mention also appeared on the scene. In 1876, Leopold Schmitt arrived in Butte, Montana's metropolis, where the mines were

Above: *Nicholas Kessler was born in Beaufort, Luxembourg, in 1833 and immigrated to the Montana Territory, where he took over Charles Beehrer's Helena brewery in 1865. He went on to become an important figure in Montana business and civic life. He died in 1901, but his name was revived for a Helena microbrewery that was started in 1982.* Author's illustration

regarded as the "richest hill on earth." Schmitt's aptly named Centennial Brewery was Butte's first major brewery and a major success story. During the 1890s, Schmitt's travels took him to Washington State, where he discovered the natural artesian waters located in the little town of Tumwater, near the state capital of Olympia. He founded his Capital Brewing Company there in 1896. While Schmitt's Butte operations would not survive, his Tumwater brewery—renamed as Olympia Brewing in 1902—flourished and remained one of the West's most important breweries through most of the twentieth century.

Whereas Butte Special claimed to be "Montana's Finest Beer," Highlander claimed to be "Montana's Favorite." Highlander was the flagship brand of the Missoula Brewing Company, which dated back to the brewery founded by George Gerber in 1874. Part of Emil Sick's Seattle-centered empire from 1944 to 1949, Missoula Brewing also did business as "Highlander Brewing" from 1949 until its demise in 1964. Bill Yenne

Above: *Francis Xavier Matt I began operating the West End Brewing Company in Utica, New York, in 1888. The company flourished during the twentieth century with its popular Utica Club lager. Five generations later, the family-owned company, now known as F.X. Matt Brewing, is going strong in the twenty-first century.* F.X. Matt Brewing via author's collection

Right: *This 1911 photo of the Heileman Brewing bottle shop shows that the company employed a large number of women. Indeed, when Gottleib Heileman passed away in 1878, it was Johanna Heileman who took over management of the LaCrosse, Wisconsin, brewery.* Author's collection

A short day's ride north of Tumwater, Seattle was quickly growing into Washington's major city. A.B. Rabbeson's Washington Brewery became the city's first brewery in 1854. It became the Seattle Brewery in 1872 and survived until 1888. By this time, a number of other brewers had arrived on the scene. The operation started by John Kopp and Andrew Hemrich in 1883 became Seattle Brewing & Malting. Best known as "The House of Hemrich," it swallowed up five other Seattle breweries between 1892 and 1904. Between 1906 and 1915, the company developed the well-known brand name Rainier, which would become a household word throughout the Pacific Northwest after Prohibition.

After growing into a metropolis as a result of the 1849 Gold Rush, San Francisco had developed a reputation for its self-sufficient citizenry. Until the completion of the Transcontinental Railroad in 1869, they were cut off from the rest of the United States by a treacherous ocean voyage that could take up to half a year.

Self-reliance meant that San Francisco had become a brewing center of importance rivaling that of Cincinnati and St. Louis. Some of San

Above: *This company photo shows the executive suite at Seattle Brewing & Malting as it appeared around 1906. The photo can be dated by the various ephemera scattered about the office containing the Rainier brand name, which was used by the company until 1915. After Prohibition, Rainier became a household word for beer lovers in the region.* Author's collection

Left: *Here, the imposing redbrick Stock House at the Heileman Brewing Company in LaCrosse, Wisconsin. Note that the brewery wagon in the foreground bears the legend "Old Style Lager," which remained the company's flagship brand for a century.* Author's collection

Above: *In 1861, Charles E. Hansen and John F. Glueck started their National Brewery at the corner of Fulton and Wester in San Francisco. John's widow, Elizabeth Glueck, succeeded him in 1877. However, by 1880, Hansen was the sole owner. The site was later home to the Acme Brewery.* San Francisco History Center via author's collection

Top right: *Adolph Nehls, a Milwaukee bartender with a quarter-century of service behind him when this photo was taken, serves up eight steins of fresh lager. At the turn of the century it was typical for brewing companies to operate numerous taverns throughout the city in which they were situated. San Francisco History Center via author's collection*

Francisco's notable breweries included those started by Charles Wilmot on Telegraph Hill in 1856 and John Wieland's Philadelphia Brewery on Second Street, which was founded the same year. The latter became John Wieland Brewing in 1887, and it was one of the West's most important breweries by the turn of the century.

Another prominent San Francisco brewing company was the National Brewery, established by John Glueck and Charles Hansen at Fulton and Webster in 1861, which would achieve a great deal of fame in the middle twentieth century for its well-known Acme brand.

It is interesting to note that, while Eastern breweries were often named after cities and regions in Germany and Central Europe, breweries in the West often were named after brewing centers in the East. San Francisco had a "Philadelphia Brewery" and, like Denver and other Western cities, San Francisco had a "Milwaukee Brewery." San Francisco's Milwaukee Brewery on Seventh Street was started in 1868 and, after surviving Prohibition, was restarted in 1935 and renamed the San Francisco Brewing Corporation.

In the years leading up to and following the turn of the twentieth century, a series of large mergers in the nation's regional brewing companies was the big industry news. In 1889, the attempt by a British investment firm to merge Pabst, Schlitz, and Blatz failed in Milwaukee, but that same year a British holding company succeeded in consolidating no fewer than eighteen St. Louis breweries into an entity called the St. Louis Brewing Association. The following year, a half-dozen companies in New Orleans were merged, and in 1901 ten Boston-area companies became the Massachusetts Breweries Company. At the same time, sixteen independent brewing companies in Baltimore—led by a "Big Three"—merged as the Gottlieb-Bauernschmidt-Straus

This group photo, circa 1890, features the staff of John Wieland's Brewery in San Francisco. Most of the employees who were included in the photo were brewery wagon drivers. The labels on the kegs touted the brewery's in-house bottling line. San Francisco History Center via author's collection

Bottom left: *In 1856, John Wieland started his Philadelphia Brewery in San Francisco and soon became one of the city's leading brewmasters. In 1887, two years after he died in a fire, the company was renamed the John Wieland Brewing.* Author illustration

Bottom right: *The Hudepohl Brewing Company was one of the largest in Cincinnati, Ohio, for many decades. It evolved from the old Buckeye Brewery that was bought by Ludwig Hudepohl and George Kotte in 1885. Kotte died in 1893 and Ludwig "Louis" Hudepohl II bought out his widow in 1900. At that point, the "Hudepohl" name was spelled out in bricks in the brewery smokestack, and the name was on its way to becoming a Cincinnati icon.* Bill Yenne

Brewers of the popular Golden State Beer, the Milwaukee Brewery in San Francisco was one of the first breweries in the West to trade in its horse-and-wagon teams for trucks. Because of the name's cachet, there would be "Milwaukee" breweries in nearly a dozen states. San Francisco History Center via author's collection

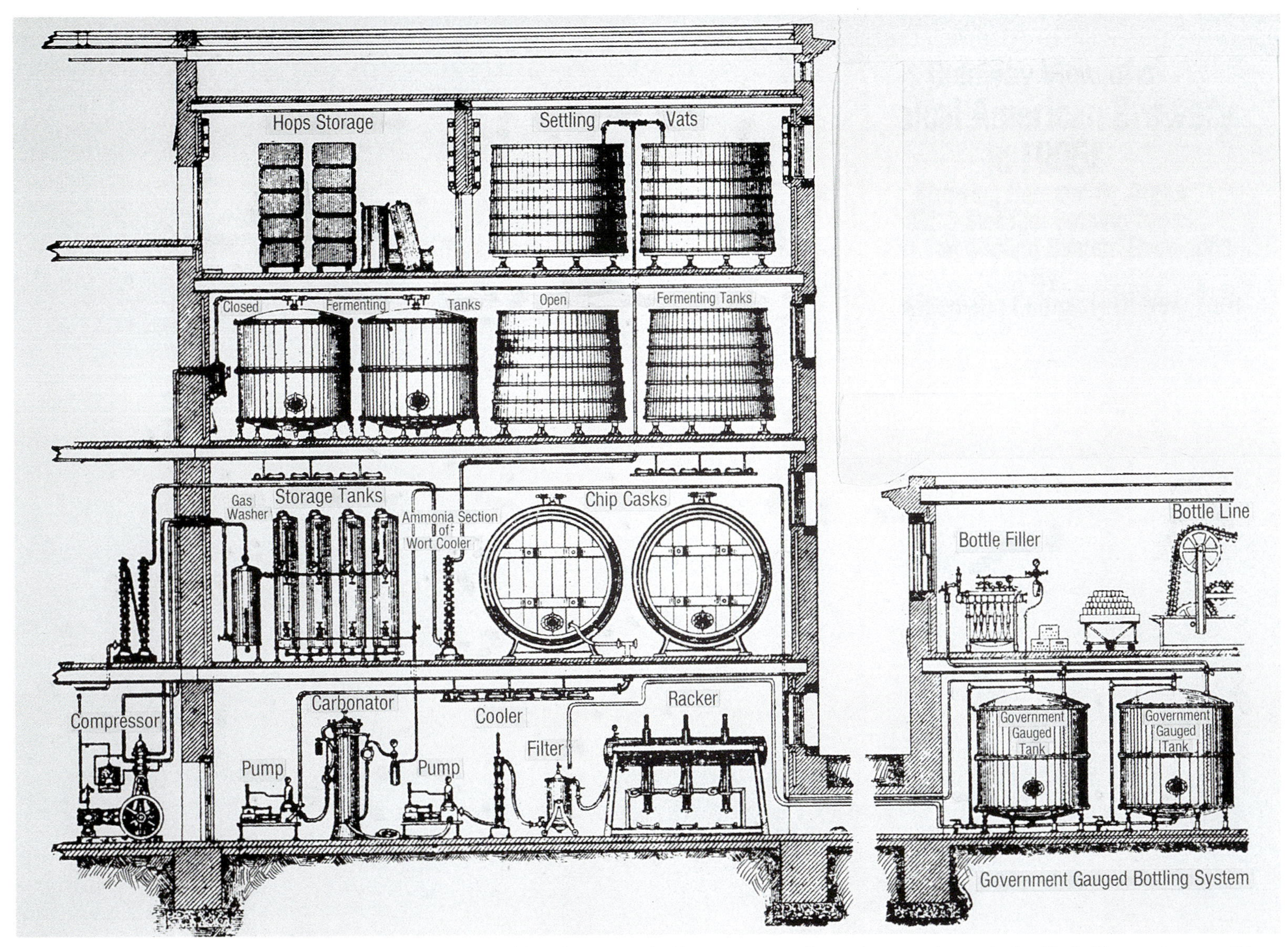

This cross section of a typical American Brewery from the 1900 to 1905 period shows fermenting and cold storage areas served by a cooling system that was developed by the Witteman Company of New York City. The bottling area on the right is fed from fermentation tanks that were federally gauged for tax purposes. Federal tax was calculated by volume, and volume was measured after final fermentation. Author's collection

Brewing Company. However, the biggest news came from Pittsburgh. In 1899, an incredible 21 brewing companies were combined to form the Pittsburgh Brewing Company. Just six years later, in reaction to the 1899 merger, fifteen more companies in Pittsburgh combined to become the Independent Brewing Company.

The United States brewing industry expanded tremendously in the half-century after the Civil War, mirroring the economy of the nation as a whole. The megabrewers in major centers such as Milwaukee and New York City grew, as did the robust regionals from San Francisco to New Orleans. However, even as this was occurring, the dark clouds of Prohibition were gathering on the distant horizon and drawing near.

Chapter 6: Prohibition and Recovery 1920–1945

Now just a distant memory, Prohibition was an earthquake that decimated both an industry and a great cultural tradition—the hometown brewer. Today regarded as one of the worst legislative disasters in United States history, Prohibition was undertaken with respectable intentions and was even described at the time as "The Noble Experiment."

It had been a long time coming, but the move toward Prohibition began gaining momentum in the late nineteenth century. Originally a religious-based sentiment, it became political as various radical organizations, such as the notorious Anti-Saloon League, became involved. Operating under the banner of the so-called "temperance movement," they demanded that government take a role in regulating personal interests.

In 1893, The Anti-Saloon League was founded in Oberlin, Ohio, by Reverend Howard Hyde Russell, representatives of various temperance societies, and evangelical, anti-Catholic churches. Later spearheaded by James Cannon Jr., a Methodist bishop, the League turned the temperance flame into a bonfire that destroyed the livelihoods of many of the families it was claiming to save. In Milwaukee alone, at least 6,500 brewers would lose their careers.

Because beer and wine were associated with immigrant cultures—especially Germans, Irish, Italians, and Catholics—there was a decidedly bigoted dimension to the temperance movement. For example, the movement often suggested that alcohol was an indulgence of inferior races. If only Washington and Jefferson had been around to rebut this notion.

Opposite: *Looking quite forlorn, this group of Florida state officers was tasked with enforcing Prohibition and confiscating liquor and beer. One can imagine that the caps on the beer bottle posed next to the man in the center, and those in the hand of the man on the right, did not remain on the bottles long after this picture was taken.* Florida State Archives via author's collection

Temperance songs were typically tearjerkers. Archibald Scott's "The Wife's Lament" mourns a heartbroken wife whose husband has fallen victim to drink. Library of Congress via author's collection

THE

WIFE'S LAMENT.

A NEW TEMPERANCE SONG

By ARCHIBALD SCOTT.—Air : Dear Irish Boy.

My Connor was loving, gentle and kind,
The proudest of mortals was I in his love,
While nature's sweet graces adorn'd his mind,
Bright angels seem'd smiling on us from above.
CHORUS.
Sweetly we started, no two more light hearted,
Together cross'd over the ocean of life ;
By true love united, the vows that he plighted
Were music the sweetest to his loviug wife.

No husband was kinder, no father e'er cherish'd
A child with a purer or holier care,
But alas ! he is chang'd, those joys are all perish'd,
Our once happy home, the abode of despair.
CHORUS.
Swearing and tearing, his acts over-bearing,
Embitter'd for ever is my future life.
The vows that he plighted are broken and slighted,
Which leaves me to mourn a heart-broken wife.

The money he once felt so proud to bestow
On home and its comforts, in days that are fled,
For rum, in the ale house, now weekly must go,
While his children are naked and starving for bread.
Chorus.—Swearing, &c.

Would I had died, ere his fall and dishonour
Enshrouded us all in a mantle of shame,
Ere rum, cursed rum ! destroy'd my poor Connor,
And quench'd in his heart love's exquisite flame.
Chorus.—Swearing, &c.

The poison that kills both the body and soul,
Has sunk him beneath they beasts of the plain.
His children and wife he forsakes for the bowl,
That has kill'd more than ever in battle was slain.
Chorus.—Swearing, &c.

405

H. DE MARSAN, Publisher.
Songs, ballads, toy-books,
60 Chatham str. New-York.

A long-suffering mother gazes away, possibly toward a sleeping child, as her husband passes out at the kitchen table, on the cover of "The Poor Drunkard's Child" by George Lowell Austin and C.A. White, which was published in 1871. Library of Congress via author's collection

SWINGIN' TO THE TEMPERANCE MOVEMENT'S GOLDEN OLDIES

The temperance movement's propagandists created a colorful picture of idyllic family life destroyed by drink. The movement spawned a celebrated songwriting boom that fed the fire by creating mournful melodies showing how miserable a life a tippler might lead. Among the more memorable were Don't Drink Any More; Don't Drink, My Boy; Tonight, Everybody Wants a Key to My Cellar; I Never Knew I Had a Wonderful Wife Until the Town Went Dry; Nowhere To Go; Pity Me Stranger; Purity, Redeemed; Tolling Sadly Tolling! (The Drunkards Funeral); Vile Wine-Cup; I Ne'er Can Forget Thee; *and the song that is perhaps the ultimate temperance anthem,* Lips That Touch Liquor Shall Never Touch Mine.

An often-abused temperance tune theme was that of fathers who destroyed their families by drinking beer. Songs that dealt with poor dad's having failed as a provider when he succumbed to demon alcohol included The Child's Lament, The Drunkard's Poor Child, The Drunkard's Daughter, When Father Comes Home, O Mother, Dear Mother, Come Home, Father! ('Tis the Song of Little Mary), *and* Father's Come Home, *the sequel to* Come Home, Father!

Of course, the temperance movement also had its own self-promoting songs, including the likes of O, Come and Sign the Pledge, The Temperance Army, The Temperance Cause is Growing, The Temperance Crusade, The Temperance Crusader, The Temperance March, The Temperance Marseillaise Hymn, *and the stirring* We Will Vote As We Pray.

U.S. Highway 61 revisited in the dark days of Prohibition. This August 1931 photo shows the Stock House at the Heileman Brewing Company in LaCrosse, Wisconsin, during the period when "cereal products" replaced Old Style Lager. Author's collection

Carrie Nation was one of the most colorful—and violent—of temperance advocates. She believed that she had been given a divine mission to destroy saloons with an ax, and her violence in the service of achieving Prohibition presaged the violence that came with Prohibition. She did not live to see Prohibition become a reality in the United States. Library of Congress via author's collection

Left: *Home and family were the theme of* Bright Sunbeams, *an 1875 collection of temperance tunes that a wife could pick out on the piano while whiling away the hours waiting for her husband to stagger home from the saloon. Among the songs in the collection was "The Temperance March" by Carl Wagner.* Library of Congress via author's collection

Workers inspect fermenting tanks at Gunther's Brewery in Baltimore, Maryland, shortly after the end of Prohibition in 1933. Founded as Gunther Brewing in 1900 by George Gunther, the company survived Prohibition as Gunther Manufacturing. The revived Gunther Brewing was eventually acquired by Hamm's in 1959. Library of Congress via author's collection

Above: *Detroit police inspect equipment discovered in a clandestine basement brewery. During Prohibition, such activity was illegal and home brewing remained a legally touchy subject for half a century.* National Archives via author's collection

Eventually, Prohibition helped revive the Ku Klux Klan, which had flourished immediately after the Civil War but had become moribund by the turn of the century. Glad to be active again, Klansmen energetically climbed aboard the bandwagon to campaign against Catholics and others they claimed were ethnically predisposed to corruption by "loose morals." In the South, alcohol abuse was often seen as the catalyst for African-American "misbehavior."

Carrie Moore Nation was one of the most colorful—and violent—temperance advocates. Born in Kentucky in 1846, she married a Missouri doctor named Charles Gloyd when she was 21 years old. When he turned out to be an alcoholic, she left him in about 1869 for a traveling evangelist. In 1877, she married David Nation, an itinerant preacher. By 1900, Carrie, like many of history's notorious fanatics, began hearing voices and came to believe that she had been given a divine assignment to destroy saloons—literally. She turned from attending prayer meetings to attacking taverns with an ax.

Nation relocated to New York City, which then, like today, was a media hub. In New York, she was able to attract the sort of attention that she craved. Standing six feet tall and weighing nearly 200 pounds, she was a forbidding figure when she rampaged into an establishment, violently breaking up furniture and glassware.

Though most temperance organizations kept her at arm's length, the media made her the poster child for the movement. Later, when she also took up the cause of women's suffrage, the mainstream groups shied away from her. She died in 1911, eight years before the nation officially adopted Prohibition and nine years before women earned the right to vote in the United States.

Some states had passed various forms of restrictive legislation during the nineteenth century, but by the early twentieth century, Prohibition became a national political issue. By 1912, the American

Assistant Secretary of the Treasury and "Prohibition czar" Lincoln C. Andrews (left) pauses outside the nation's Capitol with Commissioner of Prohibition Roy C. Haynes. They were on their way to an appearance before the Ways and Means Committee of the House of Representatives, circa 1926. Library of Congress via author's collection

Prohibition officers raiding
the Lunch Room of 922 Pa. Ave
Wash. D.C. 23792 4/25/23.

With press cameras alerted in advance, Prohibition officers stage a dramatic raid on patrons enjoying a beer with their lunch. This raid, on April 25, 1923, occurred in a dining room at 922 Pennsylvania Avenue—seven blocks from the White House in Washington, D.C. Library of Congress via author's collection

brewing industry had enjoyed a sixty-fold increase in production since the Civil War, producing 4.2 million barrels annually. With temperance coming on as a major political force, the industry would experience a sudden drop in annual production to 2.2 million barrels in 1918.

During World War I, the brewing industry was increasingly targeted by ethnic bigotry. Prohibitionists used anti-German sentiment against the owners of breweries, mainly in the upper Midwest, most of whom were German. The radicals also used the need to keep factory workers sober as an excuse to promote their agenda. German-Americans working in the brewing industry, even those whose parents were born in the United States, were openly derided as traitors for producing "Kaiser Brew."

From July 6 though 9, 1915, the Anti-Saloon League of America gathered at Atlantic City, New Jersey, for their sixteenth convention. This panoramic photo captures what was then a growing army of "drys." For an organization that touted the virtues of home and motherhood, the group had a paucity of women on their board. Library of Congress via author's collection

A young woman demonstrates the origin of the term "bootlegger" in this January 1922 photo. Typically, "bootlegs," also known as "Russian boots", were used for harder stuff than beer. Library of Congress via author's collection

Below: *After eleven miserable years of Prohibition, the "Noble Experiment" was finally seen as the catalyst for a level of violence that society had not previously known outside the Civil War. On November 16, 1922, this vehicle loaded with "moonshine" wrecked in a high-speed chase with the police.* Library of Congress via author's collection

In December 1917, bowing to Prohibitionist pressure, the United States Congress passed a Constitutional amendment to prohibit the manufacture and sale of alcoholic beverages in the United States and submitted it to the states for ratification. By then, two dozen states had already gone "dry."

A radical cult was changing the landscape of a nation. Ratified as the Eighteenth Amendment, Prohibition became law in January 1920 and was enforced by the draconian Volstead Act of 1919. Under Prohibition, it became illegal to manufacture, transport, or sell alcoholic beverages, including beer and wine, in the United States.While forcing many family businesses—from the breweries of Wisconsin to the vineyards and wineries of California—out of business, the Volstead Act unleashed a wave of organized crime, the likes of which had never previously been seen. Throughout the 1920s, bootleggers and crime kings such as Alphonse "Al" Capone of Chicago virtually ruled many American cities. The Roaring Twenties roared with illegal booze and the sound of Thompson submachine guns.

While small hometown brewers simply closed, many of the larger brewing companies turned to other products. The owners of malting facilities were able to convert to cereal products. Others turned to brewing nonalcoholic "near beer." Because real beer was never far from near beer, a tongue-in-cheek slogan cropped up: "Near Beer Sold Here. Real Beer Sold Near Here," illustrating the fact that, while legitimate businesses suffered, illegal production was rampant.

Each of the major companies vigorously promoted their own brands of near beer. Anheuser-Busch had Bevo, Miller marketed Vivo, and Coors, one of the only brewers left in Colorado, chose the auspicious name, Mannah. Schlitz, banned from brewing "The Beer That Made Milwaukee Famous," hoped to make the city famous with a product it called Famo. Pabst, meanwhile, trademarked three peculiar brand names: Hoppy, Pablo, and Yip.

In an industry that tended toward names ending in the letter "o," some of the same names were used by distantly separated regionals: Both Stroh in Detroit and Weinhard in Oregon used the name Luxo.

Ironically, the Roaring Twenties were also a boom time for soft drinks. Anheuser-Busch produced a coffee-flavored Kafo and a chocolate-flavored Carcho. Hudepohl produced root beer and Coors became a giant in the malted milk industry.

With the onset of the Great Depression in 1929, it was clear to the nation that the "Noble Experiment" had become an ignoble disaster. Gradually, Prohibition began to crumble. As early as 1926, Montana became the first of several states to repeal its state prohibition enforcement law.

In 1932, a plank in Franklin D. Roosevelt's presidential campaign platform called for "Repeal." He won in a landslide. Within a month of his inauguration in 1933, he signed "emergency" legislation legalizing beer. Though Repeal was not fully implemented through the Twenty-first Amendment until December 1933, Roosevelt "got the beer flowing" in April.

The failed effort to legislate morality had hit small businesses the worst. The major companies that had stayed afloat with near beer and other products were able to resume brewing within a short time, but smaller businesses found resumption to be a bit more difficult. Many of the small-town breweries that had folded could not resurrect their businesses. Of the 1,568 breweries that had existed in 1920, only 756 reopened, and most of these ceased to exist during the ensuing Great Depression. Because of the weight of expenses

Above: *A group of young ladies counts ballots cast in an unofficial vote regarding Prohibition "Blue Laws." The Washington-based National Liberal Alliance, not to be confused with the post-Communist Romanian political party of the same name, sponsored the balloting. When this photograph was taken on February 3, 1923, women had been able to vote in national elections for less than three years.* Library of Congress via author's collection

Left: *In a dramatic photo op staged to underscore official support for Prohibition, Mayor W. Hurd Clendenin of Zion City, Illinois, emptied two 16-ounce bottles of beer on the ground. They were just part of an 80,000-unit shipment destroyed in one afternoon.* Library of Congress via author's collection

Right: *A young woman identified as Grace Knippen showed little enthusiasm for the task at hand when she was asked to smash a bottle of Miller High Life during the media event staged by Prohibition supporters in Zion City, Illinois.* Library of Congress via author's collection

Below: *Colonel Jacob Ruppert took over the family brewery on Third Avenue in New York City and built his company into an institution. In 1915, he became owner of the New York Yankees, which he also built into an institution.* Author illustration

It was on a rainy November day in 1940 when this trio was photographed relaxing with fluted glasses of draft beer in Art's Sportsmen's Tavern in Colchester, Connecticut. The attire of the man at left suggests that he may be a mill worker. On the other hand, one might imagine these gentlemen swapping yarns after a fishing trip. Library of Congress via author's collection

incurred in reopening, many breweries that had restarted failed during the first year after Repeal.

The industry that reopened in 1933 and 1934 was clearly older and wiser. As at the time of the Civil War, leading brewers clearly saw the need to organize for the protection of their industry. New professional associations and business organizations that had formed throughout the country merged in 1941 as the United States Brewers' Association.

Just as the trade groups joined forces, so did many of the brewers. The trend toward mergers, seen at the turn of the century, resumed as a reaction to the economy. The Great Depression took a terrible toll on all aspects of society.

At the same time, the brewing companies began to explore new technology. Originally, beer had been tapped from barrels to be poured into glasses in taverns or buckets for job sites. During the nineteenth century, bottled beer had become common. By 1935, advances in packaging led brewers to begin canning beer. Krueger Brewing of Newark, New Jersey, was the

Far Right: *During World War II, getting beer to the boys overseas was the patriotic duty of American brewers. In November 1944, U.S. Navy–enlisted personnel enjoyed a beer break on Mog Mog Island in the South Pacific. The man in the center is drinking a bottle of Hudepohl, which was brewed in Cincinnati.* National Archives via author's collection

A 1920 advertisement for Minnehaha Pale depicts an Indian maid glancing away warily. With the advent of Prohibition, the Golden Grain Juice Company revived the "Minnehaha Pale" brand name for a nonalcoholic beverage. Author's collection

Above: *In April 1943, Esther Bubley photographed these two servicemen from Walter Reed Army Hospital enjoying several glasses of beer at the Sea Grill in Washington, D.C. During World War II, Christian Heurich Brewing was the only brewery still operating within the District of Columbia. Much of the product sold in the nation's capital was probably "imported" from Maryland or more distant places. If, in fact, the men* were *patients on furlough from the hospital, this photo is a testament to the recuperative power of beer. However, the two packs of cigarettes could not have helped much.* Library of Congress via author's collection

first to use a flat-topped can that was the same shape as today's beer cans. Schlitz soon followed suit with a "cone-top" can developed by the Continental Can Company to give the impression that it was shaped like a bottle.

As had been the case before Prohibition, there were still no national brewing companies on the scale that they would grow to after World War II. Anheuser-Busch and the big Milwaukee companies would grow and expand, and brands such as Pabst from Milwaukee, Grain Belt from Minneapolis, and Anheuser-Busch's Budweiser would become common throughout the upper Midwest and Mountain West. Budweiser would also flood into the South. For the time being, however, the big regionals were still the kings in their major markets on both coasts.

In New York City, George Ehret had died in 1927, seven years into Prohibition, and left behind an estate of $40 million. In 1935, his family sold the moribund brewery site in Manhattan to Colonel Jacob Ruppert, an up-and-coming industry figure. In 1936, George's son, Louis Ehret, got back into the brewing business in Brooklyn, but he never achieved the success of his father. In 1948, he transferred his operations to the old Pallisade Brewery site in Union City, New Jersey, but it folded just two years later.

Ruppert was a colorful character who was born in 1867 to privilege on Manhattan's Upper East Side. His father's brewery, founded in the year that Jacob was born, was located on Third Avenue, not far from Ehret's big brewery. As a young man, Jacob briefly served as an aide in the New York governor's office. Because of his service, he was given the honorary rank of colonel, a title he would use for the rest of his life. By the turn of the century, the Colonel had taken over the family brewing business, which was already famous for its Knickerbocker brand. By the time that Prohibition ended, the Ruppert Brewery had joined Schaefer and Ballantine as one of the big three in the New York

Far Right: *Brewery workers conduct a round of maintenance on the rivet joint of a copper kettle. It is March 1933, and after more than a decade of being out of service, the big vessel will once again brew beer.* San Francisco History Center via author's collection

Right: *The Brewer's Code of Practice was devised to set professional standards within the industry as it reconstituted itself in the wake of Prohibition.* Author's collection

City metropolitan area, and the only one of the group still brewing in Manhattan.

Colonel Ruppert achieved his own greatest fame in New York City after he bought the New York Yankees baseball club in 1915. He turned a marginal team into a legend by hiring players such as Babe Ruth, Lou Gehrig, and, much later, Joe DiMaggio, the "Yankee Clipper." Yankee Stadium, known as the "house that Ruth built," was actually built by Colonel Jacob Ruppert.

The Yankees dominated baseball during the quarter-century that the Colonel owned the team, winning the World Series seven times. When Ruppert died on Friday the 13th in January 1939, more than 4,000 people attended his funeral at St. Patrick's Cathedral.

Like the Yankees, the Ruppert Brewery continued to flourish after the Colonel's passing. The company made a serious bid toward regional expansion

Henry Weinhard began brewing in the Pacific Northwest in 1859, and he started the Portland company that bore his name in 1852. By 1879, it was the largest in Oregon. When Henry died in 1904, his daughter took over the company. The Weinhard Brewery continued to brew until 1999. Author illustration

The Brewers'

CODE OF PRACTICE

he Brewing Industry of the United States, custodian of an art and science practiced since the beginnings of recorded history, supplies a mild beverage to the major part of our population. Beer is the bulwark of moderation and sobriety. The industry recognizes its direct responsibility to itself and to the nation to conduct its operations in accord with the desires and conscience of the American public. Members of the United Brewers Industrial Foundation, in convention assembled, representing nearly half the production of beer and ale in the United States, mutually and individually pledge themselves to the following Code of Practice:

We pledge ourselves, as citizens and as business men, to conduct our business in conformity with established laws in cooperation with the authorities.

We pledge ourselves as scientific brewers to maintain exacting high standards in the brewing and packaging of beer and ale.

We pledge ourselves, with all thoughtful citizens, to the promotion of practical moderation and sobriety.

We pledge our support to the duly constituted authorities for the elimination of anti-social conditions wherever they may surround the sale of beer to the consumer.

We pledge ourselves morally to support and encourage the great body of retailers who sell beer as law-abiding citizens and who operate legal, respectable premises.

We pledge ourselves to cooperate with the duly constituted authorities to prevent beer sales to minors, or to persons who have drunk to excess.

We pledge ourselves to truth in the advertising of beer.

We pledge ourselves faithfully to observe the provisions of this Code of Practice, convinced that beer is the nation's bulwark of moderation and sobriety.

The Louisville-brewed Oertel Brewing Company promoted its "92" brand by implying that it was an extraordinary beer that "Costs you no more than ordinary beers." The brand was named for 1892, the year that John Fred Oertel became sole owner of the company. Started by Charles Hartmetz in 1874, the company had become Hartmetz & Oertel in 1884. Brewing would cease in 1967. Author's collection

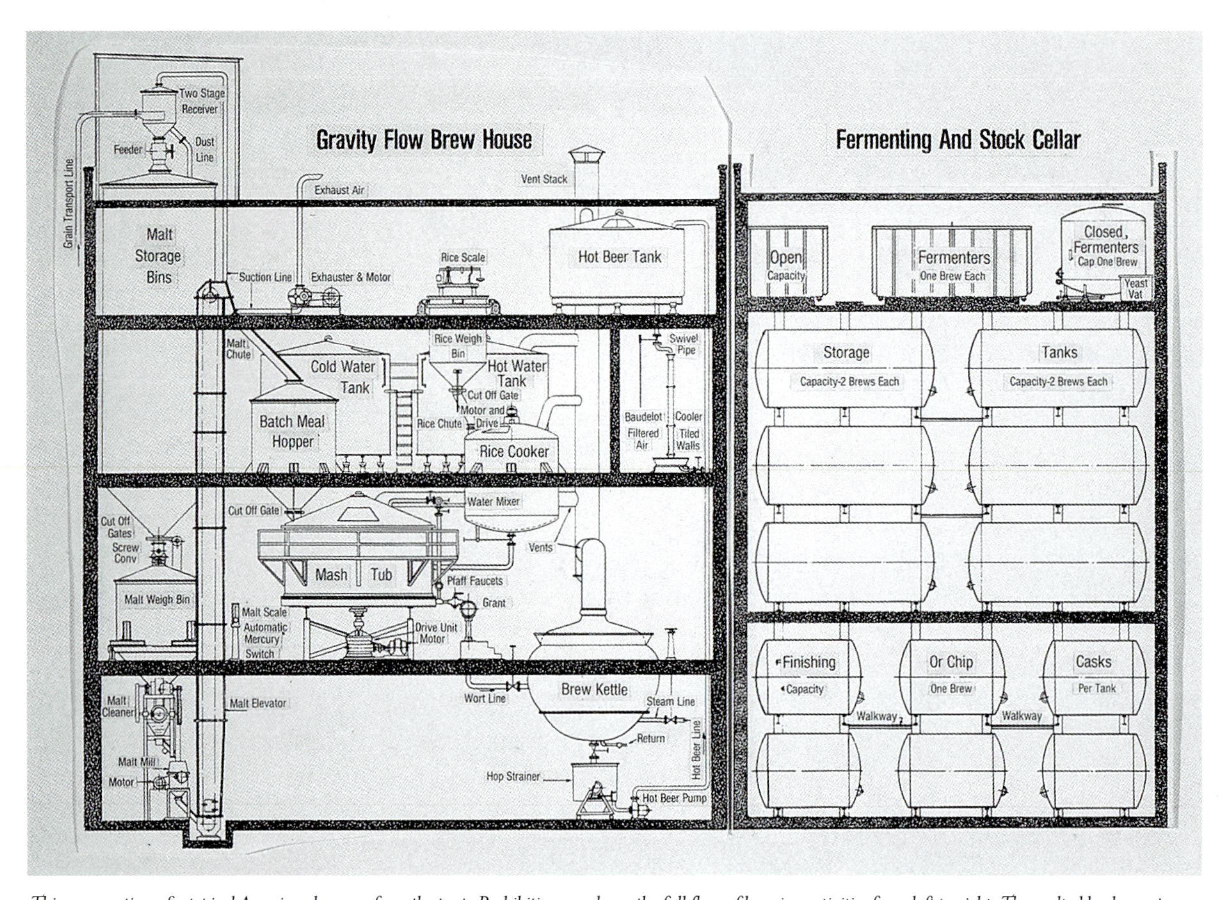

This cross section of a typical American brewery from the post-Prohibition era shows the full flow of brewing activities from left to right. The malted barley arrives at top left, is stored, and then is gravity-fed to the basement for milling. An elevator then brings it back to the top, where it passes through the mass tun (here called a "tub"), and then is fed into the brew kettle as wort. Note that by the 1930s and 1940s, brewers used rice as an adjunct. On the right side, indicated as a separate building, are the open primary fermentation tanks and the closed secondary fermentation or "lagering" tanks. Author's collection

during and after World War II with the acquisition of facilities in New York, New Jersey, Virginia, and Massachusetts. Ruppert's company even acquired the legendary New York City brand, Rheingold.

On the West Coast, the Emil Sick empire of Seattle had many similarities to the Jacob Ruppert empire in New York. Both produced a very popular beer and both were associated with a baseball team. Ruppert owned the New York Yankees of the American League from 1915 until his death in 1939. Emil Sick owned the Seattle Rainiers of the Pacific Coast League from 1938 until 1960. Of course, the notion of brewers owning baseball clubs was not confined to Ruppert and Sick. In 1953, Anheuser-Busch became the owner of the hometown St. Louis Cardinals.

Like Ruppert, Sick undertook regional expansion of his brewing enterprise—into Washington, Oregon, Montana, and the Canadian province of Alberta.

Emil Sick's father, Fritz Sick, had started the Lethbridge Brewing & Malting Company in Lethbridge, Alberta, in 1901. Emil took over from his father and used the Lethbridge brewery as a springboard for his American empire. He began by acquiring the defunct Seattle Brewing & Malting, purveyors of the well-known Rainier brand name. The company started in 1892 through the consolidation of five smaller companies, but it had folded in 1915. In 1935, before any brewing had actually started at Seattle Brewing & Malting, Sick acquired Century Brewing, which was started on Seattle's Airport Way in 1933.

Right: *Of the great California agricultural promotions of the 1940s, one of the most memorable came when the state's hop growers picked Shirley Kimball to reign as their "Queen of Hops." This fact would have been lost to time if not for the author's recent rediscovery of the film* What's Brewing, *which starred Miss Kimball. After she won first place at the California State Fair two years in a row, the Acme Brewing Company invited Kimball to tour its hop ranch near Yuba City. She apparently enjoyed taking a whiff.* AGS Historic Archives

Operating the plant as Seattle Brewing & Malting, he then re-launched the Rainier brand, which soon became a household word throughout the entire Pacific Northwest.

By 1944, Sick had two breweries operating in Seattle and had staked out a brewing empire that spanned the Northwest. He had acquired the Spokane Brewery (started by Galland-Burke in 1892) in Spokane; the Salem Brewery (started by Samuel Adolph in 1874) in Salem, Oregon;

Lucille Knutson, a young woman who happened to pass by as the photographer conducted this photo shoot, pauses to tip her hat to the San Francisco brewery, which architects of the time described as "one of the world's most beautiful industrial buildings." The photograph was taken on March 28, 1942, the day that the magnificent building officially opened. By that time, the California Brewing Association—with its Acme brand—was the largest brewer in California, with plants in both San Francisco and Los Angeles. San Francisco History Center via author's collection

Missoula Brewing (started by George Gerber in 1874) in Missoula, Montana; and the Great Falls Brewery (started in 1895 as American Brewing) in Great Falls, Montana. New brand names like Highlander (brewed in Seattle and Missoula) and Rheinlander were added to the program.

In Portland, Henry Weinhard, the grand old man of Oregon brewing, had died in 1904, but his daughter and her husband kept the company open, even after the arrival of Prohibition. In 1928, after eight years of brewing their Luxo brand's near beer, Weinhard Brewery merged with Arnold Blitz's Portland Brewing (founded in 1904) to form Blitz-Weinhard. The new company continued to operate at the Weinhard site and gradually emerged as Oregon's leading brewing company.

In California, the Acme brand was to the San Francisco Bay Area what the Rainier brand was to the Northwest. The Acme brand actually dated to 1907—the year after the Great San Francisco Earthquake—and began with the opening of the Acme Brewing Company on Sansome Street, at the foot of Telegraph Hill. In 1916, four years before Prohibition, Acme was acquired by the California Brewing Association, which had evolved from the Glueck and Hansen National Brewery, started in 1861. Reformed after Prohibition, the California Brewing Association started a satellite operation in Los Angeles in 1935, became the Acme Brewery, and was soon the largest brewing company in California.

During the 1940s, Acme's expansion plans included construction of a new brewery near the site of the old National Brewery in San Francisco. Architects described this new edifice as "one of the world's most beautiful industrial buildings."

Acme was also brewed on East 49th Street in Los Angeles from 1935 to 1954. In that year, Liebmann Breweries of New York acquired both of the Acme sites to brew their famous Rheingold brand on the West Coast. This venture ended in 1958 and the San Francisco brewery was closed, later to be demolished for a freeway off-ramp. Ownership of the Los Angeles brewery passed to

Acme employees clean and sort hops as they come down the conveyor belt. AGS Historic Archives

Left: *During the 1940s, hops were still a major agricultural crop in California, and major brewing companies owned their own fields in order to ensure an adequate supply. Acme also memorialized its hop ranch in* What's Brewing. AGS Historic Archives

the Theodore Hamm Company in 1958, and it was closed forever in 1972.

By the time the United States entered World War II in December 1941, the American brewing industry was just getting back on its feet after the twin body blows of Prohibition and Depression. Naturally, there were a few cries for a replay of the situation in 1917, when it became the policy of the United States to discourage and restrict brewing and the consumption of beer. In fact, it was proposed that service personnel should not have access to beer and that areas surrounding military installations should be rendered "dry."

To his credit, General George C. Marshall, Chief of Staff of the U.S. Army, went in exactly the opposite direction, and re-adopted the notion of a beer ration for the troops like that championed by George Washington during the Revolutionary War. Access to beer with an alcohol content of 3.2 percent was permitted on military bases, and in July 1943, the United States government actually required the brewing industry to set aside 15 percent of its production for the troops.

Unlike World War I, which served as a catalyst for Prohibition, the situation was reversed. The most critical problem faced by the United States brewing industry in World War II was how to get an adequate supply of beer to the troops overseas!

An Acme worker at the brewery in San Francisco pulls a sample for inspection. The What's Brewing *crew followed the brewing process from start to finish.* AGS Historic Archives

Left: *When she toured the Acme Brewery in San Francisco, Kimball was invited by Acme president Carl Schuster to visit his private office suite and view his personal beer stein collection. Here, he shows Kimball a stein with an Egyptian motif.* AGS Historic Archives

Blatz
FINEST BEER

CHAPTER

Consolidation and the National Brands

1945-1980

A new chapter in American brewing history began to unfold in the years immediately after World War II. To support the war effort, the United States' road and rail transportation network had been greatly enhanced. Within a few years, the construction of the vast Interstate highway system would begin, making national brands of every imaginable product—including beer—economically viable.

While the brewing industry's strategy was bold and new, the players were familiar—the two major Midwest companies, Schlitz and Anheuser-Busch.

The Joseph Schlitz Company had recognized the importance of distribution and multisite brewing at an early stage. In fact, the company had built a satellite brewery in Cleveland, Ohio, from scratch in 1908, but only operated there for two years. Anheuser-Busch, an innovator in mass distribution for over half a century, was also ready to play for a large slice of the national pie. Both companies began to look beyond national distribution and toward a truly national system of satellite breweries that was unheard of prior to World War II.

After the war, Schlitz and Anheuser-Busch took the step of building massive, new state-of-the-art breweries on both coasts. Schlitz leapt ahead when it bought Brooklyn's George Ehret Brewery in 1949. Anheuser-Busch opted to build a brand-new plant in Newark, New Jersey, which opened in 1951.

Three years later, in 1954, the two competitors became the first brewers with a coast-to-coast network of breweries, when they both opened new facilities in the Los Angeles area. Schlitz, the postwar industry leader, made its next move in 1956 by acquiring the former Muehleback Brewery in Kansas City, Missouri—right in Anheuser-Busch's backyard.

Opposite: *A very smartly dressed young lady seems to be saying "Ooooh!" as she presents a bottle of Blatz, claimed in the 1950s to be Milwaukee's "Finest."* Author's collection

Top: *The F. & M. Schaefer Brewing Company facility at the corner of Kent Avenue and South Ninth Street in Brooklyn as it appeared on a warm summer day in July 1948. The company opened its first brewery on the site in 1916. This building, built after brewing resumed in the wake of Prohibition, continued to operate until 1976.* Right: *The huge copper brew kettles at the spotlessly clean F. & M. Schaefer facility in Brooklyn as seen in February 1948. At the time, kettles such as these produced nearly 3 million barrels of beer annually, making Schaefer the fifth largest brewing company in the United States.* Library of Congress via author's collection

When photographed around the time of World War II, these huge fermenters were a new addition to Schaefer's Kent Avenue facility in Brooklyn. By mid-century, Schaefer was the fifth largest brewer in the country, but second to Ballantine in the New York City area. Library of Congress via author's collection

In 1959, both national giants opened facilities in Tampa, Florida, but by the following year, Anheuser-Busch had replaced Schlitz as America's leading brewer.

Over the course of the next twenty years, Anheuser-Busch added breweries in seven additional locations: Houston, Texas (1966); Columbus, Ohio (1968); Jacksonville, Florida (1969); Merrimack, New Hampshire (1970); Williamsburg, Virginia (1972); Fairfield, California, near San Francisco (1976); and Baldwinsville, New York (1980).

During the same period Schlitz expanded into the South with new breweries in Longview, Texas (1966); Winston-Salem, North Carolina (1970); and Memphis, Tennessee (1971). In 1964, Schlitz acquired the Hawaii Brewing Company, whose Primo Beer had a loyal cult following on the islands. Schlitz also operated the old Milwaukee Brewery in San Francisco as a Schlitz brewery between 1964 and 1969. In 1973, Schlitz consolidated its map of the United States by closing its Brooklyn and Kansas City breweries.

In 1950, Schlitz was the nation's largest brewing company with 5 million barrels of annual production, just slightly ahead of Anheuser-Busch.

Above: *Symbolic of the symbiosis between mid-twentieth-century breweries, a truck delivers new signage to taverns in Little Falls, Minnesota. The Grain Belt sign carries the phrase "The Minneapolis Beer," but both Grain Belt and Gluek's were independent Minneapolis brands. The former was the signature beer of Minneapolis Brewing; the latter was brewed by the family-owned company started by Gottleib Gluek in 1857. The six-pointed "Brewer's Star" evolved as an insignia, independently from the Star of David, and was used as the logo of the Brewer's Guild of Bohemia as early as the sixteenth century. The six points are said to represent water, hops, grain, malt, yeast, and the brewer.* Library of Congress via author's collection

By 1960, the positions were reversed, with Schlitz producing 5.6 million barrels compared to Anheuser-Busch's 8.5 million.

Pabst was another important contender for the throne of nation's leading brewer and remained in the top four from World War II through the 1970s. As the continent's industry leader at the turn of the century, Pabst emerged from Prohibition to pioneer multisite brewing by reopening in Milwaukee and starting a new brewery in Peoria Heights, near Chicago, in 1934. After World War II Pabst had actually gotten into the New York market before either Schlitz or Anheuser-Busch, through the purchase of the Hoffman Beverage Company of Newark in 1946. But Pabst's further expansion was much slower than those of Schlitz and Anheuser-Busch. In 1958 Pabst

For nearly a century, the brand name of the Joseph Schlitz Brewing Company in Milwaukee was probably the most recognized brand of beer in the United States. Marketed under the slogan "The Beer That Made Milwaukee Famous," Schlitz was brewed in Wisconsin's largest city from 1858 (when Joseph Schlitz named the company after himself) until 1981. At its peak, the brand was brewed in eight states and available nationwide. Library of Congress via author's collection

Pittsburgh youngsters enjoy a splash on a sweltering July day before World War II. Iron City was—and still is—the flagship brand of the Pittsburgh Brewing Company. An early example of industry consolidation, the company became "The Talk of the Town" in 1899 when it was formed as a result of the merger of no fewer than 21 regional, independent brewing companies. The bashful slogan "Just a Sip at Twilight" was replaced in the 1960s by the more boisterous "Pour on the Iron." Library of Congress via author's collection

Above: *The beer signs hanging over Main Street in Sheridan, Wyoming, tell part of the story of regional consolidation as Grain Belt from Minneapolis competes with Heileman's Old Style of La Crosse, Wisconsin. Sheridan, meanwhile, did have a hometown brewery. Founded in 1880, the Sheridan Brewing Company survived until 1954, after this picture was taken. The state of Wyoming had no breweries between 1954 and 1994.* Library of Congress via author's collection

A mountain of empty cases waits restocking in the backyard at the sprawling Minneapolis Brewing Company's facility in Minnesota's largest city. By evolving from the city's original brewery, started by John (Johann) Orth in 1850, the company became the city's largest. Its flagship brand, heralded here by a pair of 3,000-square-foot beer-cap-motif murals, was one of the best-known names in the entire upper Midwest for most of the twentieth century. Library of Congress via author's collection

bought the Blatz Brewery, one of its original Milwaukee rivals. From its small number of sites, Pabst remained among the top five national brewers without expansion until 1972, when a new brewery was opened in Perry, Georgia, and 1979, when the company acquired the Blitz-Weinhard Brewery in Portland, Oregon.

Meanwhile, the megabrewers of the New York City metropolitan area—notably Ballantine, Schaefer, and Ruppert—were certainly big and powerful enough to become national brewers—*if they had wanted to*. Indeed, in 1950, Ballantine was number three nationally, and Schaefer was number five, just behind Pabst. However, it was probably for the

Frederick Schaefer began brewing in New York City for Sebastian Sommers in 1838; four years later he took over the company. Together with his brother Maximilian, Frederick built Schaefer into one of New York's great brewing companies. Author illustration

Above: *Embracing new technology, this group of young people at a tavern in Mogollon (pronounced "Muggy-own"), New Mexico, voted three-to-one for canned rather than bottled or draft beer. Introduced in 1935, canned beer quickly outsold bottled beer. The presence of Pabst in New Mexico illustrates that brand's power at mid-century.* Library of Congress via author's collection

reason of size that they did not go national. Why should they expend their energies on national expansion when they were sitting atop the hemisphere's largest beer market? They felt that they could remain regional brewers and *still* be among the biggest nationally.

In the expansive decades after World War II, Schaefer operated three satellite breweries—Albany, New York (1950–1972); Cleveland, Ohio (1961–1963); and Baltimore, Maryland (1963–1978)—to help meet the demand for the popular brew. In 1972, when the Albany facility was closed, its production was transferred to a new, ultramodern brewery near Allentown in Pennsylvania's Lehigh Valley. In 1976 Schaefer's 60-year-old Brooklyn brewery, no longer economically viable, was closed. Four years

Right: *A group enjoys beer with their lunch at a Chicago bar and grill. Two have chosen a darker draft beer, served in glasses known as schooners, while the third is drinking a very light bottled lager. The brands and types are unknown, but the sign on the back wall advertises Atlas Prager (Prague style) Beer. Known as the Bohemian Brewing Company from 1891 to 1896, Atlas operated on Blue Island Avenue in Chicago until 1962. It was a subsidiary of Drewry's of South Bend from 1951 to 1962.* Library of Congress via author's collection

The brewhouse tower and the legendary smokestack at the Pearl Brewery were San Antonio landmarks for decades. J.B. Behloradsky started the company in 1883, and the facilities were greatly expanded by the San Antonio Brewing Association in the early twentieth century. In 1952, after brewing Pearl for many years, the place officially became the "Pearl Brewery." It remained independent until 1978, when General Brewing acquired it. Even after passing to Pabst in 1988, both the Pearl name and the Pearl products remained. This grand facility continued brewing until December 2002. Bill Yenne

At mid-century, the brands from Minnesota's Twin Cities—Grain Belt, Schmidt's, and Hamm's—reached out to dominate the beer drinking landscape of the Midwest. In this photograph, a brand brewed in the state capital of Minnesota seems to overpower the state capitol building in Des Moines, Iowa. The city's last brewery, Des Moines Brewing, closed in 1916 and nothing reopened there until the microbrewery era. Library of Congress via author's collection

BREWERIANA

Americans have a peculiar interest in—some would say an "obsession with"—the artifacts of their civilization. This manifests itself in collecting. Americans are inveterate collectors. In the case of our American brewing heritage, the object of the collector is called "breweriana."

This general topic includes anything related to brewing, but centers especially on objects related to the marketing and packaging of beer. Breweriana aficionados typically collect branded artifacts that relate to a favorite brewery or a product. Foremost on the list are labels, bottles, cans, and coasters. More serious collectors search for such things as tap handles, promotional novelties, and signs. Lighted signs, including neon examples and the famous Hamm's and Olympia "waterfall" signs, are among the most highly sought. Breweriana fans also collect ephemera such as magazine advertising and souvenir booklets that were given away at brewery tours through the years.

As with other collectors, many breweriana lovers have organized themselves into clubs. Some of the most notable are the American Breweriana Association, which publishes the American Breweriana Journal, *as well as the National Association Breweriana Advertising and Beer Can Collectors of America. Many breweries, particularly fondly remembered breweries from the past, have active fan clubs and historical societies.*

Left: *The iconic Lone Star brewery in San Antonio, Texas. Established by Adolphus Busch, but never part of Anheuser-Busch, Lone Star was proudly proclaimed as "The National Beer of Texas" and it enjoyed a strong local following despite its out-of-state ownership. George Muelebach of Kansas City acquired the company during the 1940s, and Olympia owned the brewery from 1976 to 1983, when ownership passed to Heileman.* Above: *There was no arguing with this San Antonio billboard that proudly proclaimed Lone Star as "The National Beer of Texas," for long did it reign as such.* Bill Yenne

later, Schaefer became merely a brand name of Stroh and Allentown became a Stroh facility.

Ballantine closed its two Newark breweries in 1948 and 1971, then it was also reduced to a brand name. Ironically, Ballantine and Schaefer declined and were swallowed by out-of-state national brands.

Despite the moves by Anheuser-Busch and Schlitz into Southern California, the western regionals fared better than their counterparts in the Northeast during the quarter-century after World War II. Both Olympia in Tumwater, Washington, and Blitz-Weinhard in Portland were single-site brewers. On the other hand, the Emil Sick Empire—famous for the Rainier brand—and Lucky Lager, with locations throughout the West, represented postwar attempts to create multisite regional empires that paralleled the major national brands' efforts in the East. Excluding their California and Texas operations, neither Schlitz, Pabst, nor Anheuser-Busch had breweries spread over an area larger than Lucky Lager's area during its peak in the West.

The story of Lucky Lager is thoroughly intertwined with that of the General Brewing Company of Vancouver, Washington. The first Lucky Lager brewery is a case in point. Located on Newhall Street in San Francisco, it was started by General in 1934 and it carried both names off and on until it was closed in 1978.

The second Lucky brewery, at Azuza in Southern California, was started in 1949, sold to General in 1963, and then to Miller in 1966. The third Lucky brewery was located in Vancouver, Washington, and actually traced its heritage back to the brewery that Henry Weinhard had owned between 1859 and 1864. Restarted after Prohibition as the Interstate Brewery, it was sold to Lucky in 1950, to General in 1964, and back to Lucky in 1969. After General's 1971 purchase of Lucky, the Vancouver facility served as the flagship brewery until its closure in October 1985.

Throughout their long courtship, both Lucky and General established other widely dispersed satellite breweries in the West, including Los Angeles (General, 1971–1974); Pueblo, Colorado (General, 1971–1975); and Salt Lake City (Lucky, 1960–1964, and General, 1964–1967). In the case of Lucky Lager, this move helped establish it as one of the West's most important and widely recognized brand names from the mid-1950s to the mid-1980s.

Falstaff was another Midwest brewer to emerge as a national power after World War II. From the nation's seventh largest brewing company in 1950, it rose to

continued on page 97

Introduced in 1952, the Hamm's Bear is certainly the most important fictional animal in the history of brewery advertising. Credit for the Hamm's bear is given to Cleo Hovel, an art director for the Campbell Mithun agency in Minneapolis, although the bear was actually designed and drawn by illustrator Ray Tollefson. Theo. Hamm's Brewing via author's collection

Preferred... *for mellow moments*

Matching the mood of your moments of leisure, Hamm's is a beer of rare smoothness and subtle mellowness.

This has been our custom for 82 years: to malt our own prize barley, reaped in the fertile fields close by, to use crystal-clear artesian water, to brew our beer with surpassing skill under the guidance of a brewmaster who carries on the tradition for Hamm quality established by his father and grandfather.

Hamm's is preferred by millions. Today it can be your preference, too . . . because we are expanding our brewery, which already is known as one of the largest in the nation.

For your mellow moments, you too will certainly prefer Hamm's—truly the smooth and mellow beer.

This "pre-bear" advertising for Hamm's underscored the beer's presence in the "Land of 10,000 Lakes." One wonders why two bottles are being presented, even though there are three men here. Perhaps the man who caught no fish will get no beer. Author's collection

In this 1947 advertisement, Pabst clearly positioned its elite Blue Ribbon brand as a beer for the upper crust. After a long night of serving Blue Ribbon to his tony employers and their guests, the butler is having one for himself. Author's collection

In the late 1940s, Ballantine stressed its trademarked trio of rings—Purity, Body, and Flavor—in its advertising. The use of the cowboy made Ballantine seem to be an "Out West" product, despite the fact that the marketing base was within an hour's radius of New York City. You can almost feel the chill on the glass in this beautifully airbrushed illustration. Author's collection

THE GROWTH OF LEADING U.S. BREWING COMPANIES DURING THE CONSOLIDATION PERIOD

	Annual Output (Millions of Barrels)	Share of Total of United States Market
1950: The Top Five Brewing Companies		
1. Schlitz	5.1	6%
2. Anheuser-Busch	4.9	6%
3. Ballantine	4.4	5%
4. Pabst	3.4	4%
5. Schaeffer	2.8	3%
1960: The Top Five Brewing Companies		
1. Anheuser-Busch	8.5	10%
2. Schlitz	5.7	6%
3. Falstaff	4.9	6%
4. Carling	4.8	5%
5. Pabst	4.7	5%
1970: The Top Five Brewing Companies		
1. Anheuser-Busch	22	18%
2. Schlitz	15	12%
3. Pabst	10	8%
4. Coors	7	6%
5. Schaeffer	6	5%
1980: The Top Five Brewing Companies		
1. Anheuser-Busch	50	28%
2. Miller	37	21%
3. Pabst	15	9%
4. Schlitz	15	9%
5. Coors	14	8%
1990: The Top Five Brewing Companies		
1. Anheuser-Busch	80	42%
2. Miller	61	22%
3. Stroh	21	10%
4. Coors	20	9%
5. Heileman	19	8%

number three by 1960. In 1975, Falstaff, like Lucky Lager, became affiliated with General Brewing. Falstaff was started by "Papa Joe" Griesedieck, who purchased two breweries in St. Louis between 1911 and 1917. During Prohibition, the company was renamed Falstaff after the Shakespeare character, and it whiled away those years brewing near beer and smoking hams. After Prohibition, in 1933, Falstaff acquired the former Union Brewery in St. Louis, then went upriver to acquire the former Fred Krug Brewery in Omaha in 1935, and down river to New Orleans, where it purchased the former National Brewery in 1937. Falstaff emerged from World War II with more (albeit smaller) breweries in St. Louis than Anheuser-Busch. But while the latter moved forward to a truly national market, Falstaff continued to concentrate on the Mississippi/Missouri River country.

In 1952, Falstaff reached toward the rapidly expanding California market by acquiring Wieland's Brewery in San Jose, originally Gottfried Krahenberg's Fredericksburg Brewery (established in 1856), one of the first breweries in California. In doing so, Falstaff was the first major eastern brewer to expand into the Golden State, beating both Schlitz and Anheuser-Busch, who were then concentrating on the New York area, by two years.

Between 1954 and 1956, Falstaff purchased breweries in Indiana and moved into Texas—again ahead of Anheuser-Busch and Schlitz—by opening breweries in El Paso and Galveston. Falstaff also moved deeper into California, briefly operating two breweries in San Francisco, including the former Lucky Lager Brewery on Newhall Street.

By 1960, the fourth largest brewing company in the United States was actually Canadian. Carling, then Canada's third largest brewery, had made its first inroads in the United States before World War II through the Brewing Corporation of America—Carling Brewing Company after 1953—in Cleveland, Ohio. In 1954, Carling acquired the former Griesedieck Western breweries, which were famous for their Stag Beer brand, in Belleville, Illinois, and St. Louis. Henry Griesedieck, who was a cousin to Falstaff's Griesediecks, owned the company.

In 1956 Carling added breweries in Natick, Massachusetts, and in Frankenmuth, near Detroit,

continued on page 100

Apparently the mere sight of his smiling, rosy-cheeked wife had not caused our hero to eschew the evening paper. She has the solution, the gateway to any man's heart—lager. Items of note in this 1946 advertisement are the fact that Schlitz pictures its can alongside the bottle, at the lower right, as well as their promise that the beer had "none of that harsh bitterness." Already, the industry was preparing consumers for its retreat from using large quantities of hops.
Author's collection

As World War II ended, Schlitz proudly announced that it was now delivering the beer of the future. Schlitz promised that during the late twentieth century people would travel the world in glass-winged jetliners, Milwaukee would be the only American city visible from near-earth orbit, and beer would have "no bitterness." None of these predictions would come to pass, of course, and Schlitz would vanish as an independent brewing company. The blandness implied by the "kiss of hops" strategy would turn out to be a kiss of another kind. Author's collection

A wholesome young lady with an enigmatic smile jealously clutches a glass of lager in a mid-1950s advertisement. Author's collection

continued from page 97

Michigan. Two years later, the Canadian-based brewer also expanded to Atlanta, Georgia, and Tacoma, Washington, creating an archipelago of breweries that made many American brewers envious.

During the early 1960s Carling opened breweries in Baltimore, Fort Worth, and Phoenix, but the latter part of the decade was marked by the company's gradual decline in the market. Business declined in the ensuing decade, and in 1979 Carling left the United States market and sold off its holdings to American companies. The famous Carling Black Label brand went to Heileman and became part of the Pabst portfolio in 1999.

The quarter-century after World War II was also the golden age of brewery advertising. One of the truly legendary brewery advertising gimmicks of all time was started almost by accident by the Liebmann Breweries of Brooklyn, brewers of the well-known Rheingold brand. In 1940, Philip Liebmann decided to use a starlet named Jinx

TOTAL U.S. MARKET SHARE CONTROLLED BY THE TOP FIVEAMERICAN BREWING COMPANIES DURING THE CONSOLIDATION PERIOD

1950:	24%
1960:	32%
1970:	49%
1980:	75%

TOTAL U.S. MARKET SHARE CONTROLLED BY THE TOP FIVE AMERICAN BREWING COMPANIES IN THE WAKE OF THE CONSOLIDATION PERIOD

1990:	91%
2000:	95%

Falkenberg in his advertising, and he dubbed her "Miss Rheingold." The response from the public was tremendous, and everyone insisted that Liebmann designate another Miss Rheingold the following year. In 1942, Liebmann had the brainstorm to let the public vote for Miss Rheingold. Throughout the 1950s, Miss Rheingold became a major sensation in the New York City area. By 1959, more than 20 million votes were cast annually

The sampler on the wall of a comfortable den cheerfully offers a tray of very translucent Pabst Blue Ribbon, poured into mugs with stylish rattan handles. One wonders how the photographer's stylist got those soapy bubbles into the bottles. Author's collection

Anheuser-Busch had been brewing in Southern California for 22 years when the company opened this big, modern Anheuser-Busch plant at Fairfield, California (near San Francisco in Northern California), in 1976. This stainless steel "grant" is located at the Fairfield facility. In the brewing process, sweet wort passes through the grant, where it is aerated and checked for clarity. Bill Yenne

for Miss Rheingold. In fact, more people in the five boroughs were voting for Miss Rheingold than were voting in presidential elections.

Liebmann's Miss Rheingolds appeared on cans of Rheingold Beer and at publicity events. Some vanished into obscurity after their reign, while others, like Jinx Falkenberg, became professional celebrities or went on to movie careers. Celeste Yarnall, Miss Rheingold of 1964, went on to star in three Elvis Presley films. It was Yarnall to whom the King sang the song "A Little Less Conversation" in the film *Live a Little, Love a Little*. Yarnall was also the last Miss Rheingold elected; Liebmann Breweries ended the Miss Rheingold phenomenon in 1965, by selecting Sharon Vaughn to reign as the last of the dynasty.

Male celebrities also pitched beer during the golden age of brewery advertising. Jim Backus, best known as Thurston Howell III on *Gilligan's Island*, was also the voice of the cartoon character, Mr. McGoo. In this guise, Backus served as a pitchman for Stag Beer.

ALCOHOL CONTENT IN BEER

The alcohol content of beer generally ranges from 4 to 6 percent by volume, with some exceptions at both ends. For example, Belgian dubbel and tripel, as well as German doppelbock and English barley wine have upwards of 8 or 9 percent by volume.

Contrary to popular misconception, color and opacity have nothing to do with alcohol content. Irish stout is probably the darkest and most opaque beer style in the world, yet its alcohol content is around 4 percent. Meanwhile, many Belgian tripels with alcohol content in excess of 8 percent are golden and translucent.

Throughout the world, the alcohol content of both beer and wine is measured by volume—except in the United States, where the content of beer is measured and regulated by weight. Technically, it is measured by specific gravity, rather than by weight, but the statutes read "weight."

In the context of beer, specific gravity is the measure of alcohol's density relative to water, and alcohol weighs less by volume than does water. Thus, the percentage of alcohol by mass is higher than its percentage by volume because an equal mass of alcohol occupies more volume than water would. Therefore, when measured "by weight," the percentage of alcohol is about 0.8 that of alcohol measured "by volume."

In the United States, the regulatory benchmark is 4 percent by volume, which translates to 3.2 percent by weight. This arbitrary number is used by many states and municipalities to regulate what alcoholic beverages may be sold in grocery stores. Typical American beer has between 3.6 and 3.8 percent alcohol, but for states with 3.2 percent laws, the major national breweries create 3.2 percent versions of their usual brands. In many places, the sale of beer that exceeds 3.2 percent by weight is prohibited—except in designated state-monopoly liquor stores. In Utah, for example, the penalties for the public sale of beer with more than 3.2 percent alcohol by weight are so great that many breweries produce 2.8 percent beer just to be on the safe side. Ironically, Utah's state-owned liquor stores are allowed to sell any type of liquor.

Other states have strange laws that have had strange consequences and have resulted in strange products. In Oklahoma, beer that exceeds 3.2 percent by weight must be called "strong beer." Under California law, beer that exceeds 3.99 percent alcohol by weight can be sold in grocery stores, but it must be labeled "malt liquor," rather than beer. As a result, some people are under the misconception that "malt liquor" is either not really beer, or that it is a legitimate beer style. As an unintended repercussion, California's law has given "malt liquor" a cache among the young by singling it out as an inexpensive source of high alcohol content.

Historically, high alcohol content has always been a selling point, especially in the wake of Repeal in the early 1930s. For this reason, the federal government banned alcohol content from labeling in 1935, although states were permitted to impose regulations of their own. Over the years, a number of state legislatures have introduced laws mandating wording on labels such as "not over 3.2 percent alcohol by weight."

Above: *No longer in operation, "Papa Joe" Griesedieck's Falstaff Brewery in St. Louis was built in the early days of the twentieth century when the city's brewing industry was expanding. For most of the century, Falstaff was one of the biggest names in American brewing. Now it is just a footnote remembered by few.* Bill Yenne

No doubt the men working on this billboard in Vincennes, Indiana, were thirsty by the time they were finished. Brewed in Fort Wayne, Berghoff was a well-known independent Midwest brand throughout most of the twentieth century. Herman Berghoff started the company in 1887 and it was sold to Falstaff in 1954. The Berghoff Restaurant in Chicago revived the name from 1991 to 1993, although the new Berghoff was actually brewed in Wisconsin by Joseph Huber. Library of Congress via author's collection

The radio comedy team of Bob Elliot and Ray Goulding, known simply as "Bob and Ray," also pitched beer as cartoon characters, adopting the personae of Bert and Harry Piel to advertise the products of the Piel Brothers Brewery of Brooklyn. The actual Piel brothers had been Gottfried, Michael, and Wilhelm, who started their company in 1883.

Yet, not all the cartoon characters that marketed beer were backed by human celebrities. The most famous and best-loved cartoon character in the history of brewery advertising had few speaking parts. The famous "Hamm's Bear" of St. Paul's Theodore Hamm Brewery was a staple of the company's image for decades, even after the brand became part of the Pabst portfolio in 1983. His public career ended

Above: *An aerial view of the Miller Brewing Company flagship plant in Milwaukee, Wisconsin, in the 1980s. The steam marks the location of the actual brewing operations. Fermentation takes place in the tanks at the right, while the trucks in the foreground mark the docks where packaged product is loaded for distribution.* Jeff Waalkes, Miller Brewing Company

only when neo-temperance agitators complained about cartoons being used to sell alcoholic beverages. The Hamm's Bear became one of the leading icons of brewery advertising lore, and is today one of the most sought-after artifacts of breweriana.

Non-animated fictional characters were also used. Seattle's Rainier Brewing featured television spots with the memorable "Brewmaster," a stern individual with shaven head and handlebar mustache. Olympia Brewing in Tumwater, Washington, used its famous artesian water as grist for television commercials. Since nobody really knew what an "Artesian" was, the spots pictured people in dark and creepy woods, listening to a distant rustling identified in a whisper as "those Artesians."

The golden age of brewery advertising also spawned great slogans. Schlitz still marketed "The Beer That Made Milwaukee Famous," and in 1966 began to assert that "When you're out of Schlitz, you're out of Beer."

Meanwhile, Miller's High Life was strangely identified as the "Champagne of Bottled Beer," and the commercials starring the Hamm's Bear also featured a memorable jingle touting Hamm's as the beer "From the Land of Sky Blue Waters."

For its customers in the Golden State, Lucky Lager coined the double entendre "It's Lucky when you Live in California." Continuing to play on the artesian water, Olympia marked its packaging with the phrase "It's the Water."

Another beer with a clever slogan and cult following that achieved prominence in the 1960s and 1970s was Lone Star. Brewed by the Lone Star Brewing Company in San Antonio, Texas, the beer developed an impassioned clientele within its home state. Immortalized in the "outlaw" country songs of Willie Nelson, Waylon Jennings, and Jerry Jeff Walker, Lone Star became reverently known as the "National Beer of Texas." It remained independent until 1976, when it was first sold and then resold to a succession of out-of-state companies, including Olympia, Heileman, Stroh, and Pabst.

By the 1970s, however, things were not all fun and games for the American brewing industry. There had been a major shakeout in the 1950s when the national brewers asserted themselves; this climate revved up again in the 1970s.

During the latter half of the decade, the bumbling presidency of Jimmy Carter saddled the United States with double-digit inflation while his lager-swilling brother, Billy, became the pitchman for his own brand of beer. As a joke,

Left: *The big, stainless steel brew kettles on the floor of the Miller Brewing Company flagship brewery in Milwaukee. The plant produces the largest proportion of the 40 million barrels brewed annually by the company.* Jeff Waalkes, Miller Brewing Company

Falls City Brewing of Louisville, Kentucky, marketed a mild lager called "Billy Beer" that was "endorsed" by the tippling presidential sibling. The short-lived gag product became a temporary collector's item. Falls City was sold to Heileman in 1978, and the Carter presidency ended in 1981.

The recession that hung over most of the 1970s like a dark cloud forced many brewers to close their doors or consolidate in order to survive. During this consolidation period, the total annual output of the industry doubled even as the number of brewing companies shriveled from over 400 in 1950 to just 140 independent brewing companies in the early 1960s. There would be fewer than fifty as the 1980s began. As in many other industries, market share was concentrated more and more in the hands of fewer and fewer companies.

The total volume of beer produced in the United States increased slightly from 83 million barrels in 1950 to 88 million in 1960, but the market share of the top ten brewing companies increased from 38 to 52 percent. For the top five, it increased from 24 to 32 percent. Between 1970 and 1980, annual output soared to 176 million barrels, but by then the top ten accounted for 93 percent, with the top five having a 75 percent market share.

Anheuser-Busch emerged as the market leader and extended its lead by building new facilities rather than by acquiring existing breweries. Elsewhere, mergers and acquisitions defined the industry. One of the most auspicious was the acquisition of Milwaukee's Miller Brewing by the Philip Morris tobacco company. Philip Morris bought a 53 percent share from the W.R. Grace Company in 1969 and purchased the remaining shares in 1970. Within a decade, Miller had risen from number seven to number two nationally.

Schlitz, the previous number two brewing company, had maintained that position for a quarter-century, while continuing to grow and outpace a succession of third-place American brewers though the 1960s and early 1970s. However, the fortunes of Milwaukee's leading company began to sink in the 1970s after it reformulated its already pale lager to be even lighter. Schlitz was able to cut production costs, but the

The huge control panel at Miller's Milwaukee brewery, circa 1970s. A marvel of postwar technology, such consoles brought scientific precision to the brewer's art and became essential equipment as the nation's major breweries became even larger. Jeff Waalkes, Miller Brewing Company

A worker on a Miller Brewing line monitors the canning of the company's venerable Miller High Life. Once the company's leading brand, it was eclipsed in the 1980s and 1990s by Lite and Genuine Draft. Jeff Waalkes, Miller Brewing Company

The phrase "Let there be Lite" comes to mind when describing this vintage scene from the early days after the Miller Brewing Company introduced its reduced-calorie favorite. When Lite went on the market in 1975, it became an industry phenomenon and Miller's best-selling beer. Jeff Waalkes, Miller Brewing Company

public perception was that Schlitz was also cutting the quality of the beer. Even as the company invested in a nationwide plant expansion program, sales declined.

The end of the road was in sight in 1976, when Schlitz was forced to dump a large quantity of beer that was deemed defective. The company would never recover. An event symbolic of the times for Schlitz came in 1979, with the sale of its two-year-old Baldwinsville, New York, brewery to Anheuser-Busch.

By 1981, Schlitz was on the ropes and entertaining buyout offers from Pabst and G. Heileman. The latter won the bidding, but the United States Justice Department nixed the deal on antitrust grounds. A year later, Stroh Brewing of Detroit made an offer that pleased the feds and closed the Schlitz plant in Milwaukee. In a further bit of irony, Stroh would close its own Detroit brewery in 1985.

Meanwhile, Falstaff and the affiliated General Brewing Company (Lucky Lager), had closed all of their California plants by 1978 (the San Jose brewery was closed in 1973), and all of its St. Louis plants by 1977, leaving their New Orleans, Omaha, and Ft. Wayne plants as the lone brewers under the Falstaff name. In the meantime, Falstaff had acquired Ballantine in 1972 and Narragansett in 1965. The Narragansett Brewing Company in Cranston, Rhode Island, had been established in 1890 and had become a popular brand name in New England. For this reason, Falstaff briefly continued operations under the Narragansett name. In 1978, General acquired Pearl Brewing in San Antonio, Texas.

Between 1983 and 1985, the Ballantine, Falstaff, General, Lucky Lager, Narragansett, and Pearl

Rows of massive fermentation tanks in the cool cellar of a major lager producer. The light lager favored by the major brewing companies may spend up to eight weeks fermenting in a place such as this before it is packaged. Bill Yenne

Pabst brewery trucks, lined up and ready for action in the summer of 1954. The "Blue Ribbon" insignia is clearly visible on the doors, and it is repeated in the advertising tie-in posters for the Gary Merrill–Jan Sterling movie that's coming soon. Author's collection

Right: *This dramatic brewery-top installation from the 1960s was animated with neon tubing so that the Hamm's glass would be "filled" and "refilled" with yellow light, and ultimately capped with white "foam." At its apogee in the postwar years, Minnesota-based Hamm's operated brewing facilities from Maryland to California.* San Francisco History Center via author's collection

brands and breweries were all acquired by the S&P holding company, which was owned by the enigmatic Paul Kalmanovitz. This and the demise of Schlitz were only two rounds in a quick series of consolidations that would cause most of the great brand names from the history of American brewing to cease operations as independent entities by the mid-1980s.

Hamm's had been acquired by Olympia in 1975, which, in turn, would be acquired by Pabst in 1983. Two years later, all three names became part of the S&P portfolio as Kalmanovitz added Pabst to his previous holdings.

Meanwhile, another blizzard of consolidations was blowing in from Wisconsin—not Milwaukee, but LaCrosse. The G. Heileman Brewing Company was then a unique example of a small regional brewer that grew to national prominence, not through the vehicle of a single national brand, but through an amazing amalgam of important, formerly independent, regional brands that Heileman continued to brew under their original names.

In 1960, Heileman was the thirty-first largest brewer in the United States, but by 1982 it was fourth. One of its first major acquisitions was its purchase of Blatz—one of the Big Four names in Milwaukee—from Pabst in 1969. In 1979, Heileman acquired four former Carling National breweries in the United States from the Canadian brewing giant, including the former Griesedieck Western breweries in Belleville, Illinois, and St. Louis. Along with the acquisition, Heileman picked up the Griesedieck's popular Stag brand and a license to brew Carling's Black Label and Red Cap Ale.

In reviving the Blatz name, Heileman went to the unusual length of creating a retro-style microbrewery on 10th Street in Milwaukee to brew the beer and market it against the backdrop of Milwaukee brewery nostalgia. The Val Blatz 10th Street Brewery opened in September 1986.

The Burgermeister building at 470 Tenth Street in San Francisco as it appeared in 1951. When it was built, it was the largest brewing facility west of St. Louis, with nearly a one-million-barrel capacity. It was a Falstaff plant from 1975 until 1978, when it was closed permanently. San Francisco History Center via author's collection

As is suggested by the Blatz and Carling acquisitions, Heileman did not achieve its growth by simply buying no-name breweries in out-of-the-way places. Rather, Heileman specifically acquired the *signature* regional brewing companies in a number of regions. Indeed, Heileman's own house brand, Heileman Old Style, had a wide regional following, especially in Chicago. In 1976, Heileman also bought the Grain Belt brand of Minneapolis, later acquired Jacob Schmidt Brewing from across the river in St. Paul, and then consolidated their operations. (In 1991, Heileman would sell the Grain Belt name and the Schmidt St. Paul brewery to the Minnesota Brewing Company.)

In the early 1980s, Heileman went west to acquire Rainier, which Emil Sick had made into the signature beer of Seattle, as well as Portland's mythical Blitz-Weinhard Company. In 1983, Heileman also bought the Lone Star Brewing Company of San Antonio, makers of the self-styled "National Beer of Texas," which had been owned by Olympia since 1976.

In 1987, Heileman was acquired by Alan Bond of Australia, whose holdings constituted one of the world's largest multinational companies, including the Swan Brewery and the Pittsburgh Brewing Company, which brewed Iron City, the signature brand of western Pennsylvania.

Smaller consolidations also formed local conglomerates. A case in point occurred in Cincinnati, where Hudepohl and Schoenling merged in 1988 to form Hudepohl-Schoenling, which operated under the slogan—if not the official name—of "Cincinnati's Brewery."

Worth a passing mention are two long-lived regional family brewers who survived the consolidation period to reach the turn of the twenty-first century as major players on the national brewery scene: August Schell of New Ulm, Minnesota, founded in 1860, and Yuengling of Pottsville, Pennsylvania. Founded in 1829, Yuengling is today the oldest brewing company in the United States.

A third company that also fits the profile of a long-surviving family regional is Jones Brewing of

The August Schell Brewery of New Ulm, Minnesota, seen here in July 1974, was typical of the tiny, family-owned breweries that fell by the wayside in the quarter-century after World War II. However, the company beat the odds, not only by surviving, but also by flourishing. In 2002, little Schell came full circle by acquiring Grain Belt, which had been one of Minnesota's two biggest brands for most of the twentieth century. National Archives and via author's collection

The General Brewing/Lucky Lager draft horse team is displayed at the company's big Newhall Street brewery in San Francisco. In the decade or so after World War II, Lucky Lager's brand identity and market share in California grew faster and larger than that of Anheuser-Busch's Budweiser or any other "Eastern" brand. San Francisco History Center via author's collection

The Anheuser-Busch Clydesdale team poses with a McDonnell Douglas F/A-18A Hornet strike fighter, circa 1979. The two St. Louis-based companies were getting together for a little joint publicity. Used operationally until Prohibition, the Clydesdale team was brought back in 1933 to carry cases of Budweiser to President Roosevelt and to Governor Al Smith in New York. They were such a hit that Anheuser-Busch created permanent demonstration teams. The company still owns between 200 and 250 of the big draft horses. Author's collection

Joe Allen, the brewmaster at Anchor Brewing in San Francisco, pulls a glass of Anchor Steam Beer in January 1952. The last independent brewery in San Francisco, Anchor was scheduled to close in 1965. However, young Fritz Maytag, who had developed a fondness for the unique beer, bought the company to save it. Since then, both Anchor and Maytag have become industry legends. San Francisco History Center via author's collection

Smithton, Pennsylvania. Established in 1907 by Welsh immigrant William B. "Stoney" Jones as the Eureka Brewing Company, the brewery's original brand was Eureka Gold Crown. However, because Stoney Jones habitually made personal sales calls to taverns in the area, it was known unofficially as "Stoney's Beer." The brewery lost little time changing the official name. Until recently, it was operated under the presidency of William B. "Bill" Jones III.

The company today subscribes to the notion that "The beer most in demand is a product brewed in the traditional fashion [and] that this is why foreign or imported beers are gaining an increasing share of the market . . . as Americans become more and more disenchanted with American 'fad' beers. The Jones Brewing Company, therefore, has chosen not to get involved in fads and gadgets, but instead will brew the finest natural (or traditional) beer possible!" As late as the 1980s, the brewery closed down each year to accommodate the staff's hunting plans.

With the consolidation of the late 1970s and early 1980s came an intense competition for market share that led major brewing companies to develop a wider product line with new types of beers. Curiously, they failed to predict the paradigm that would be explored by the coming Microbrewery Revolution. Instead of creating new beers with *more* taste, the older brewing companies created beers with *less* taste. In fact, the phrase being used was "flavor neutral."

The venerable Henry Weinhard Brewery on West Burnside in Portland, Oregon, was still going strong when this photograph was taken in 1994. Eleven breweries had flourished in the city prior to 1905, but when Prohibition was repealed only this plant, now the Blitz-Weinhard Brewery, returned. It remained family-operated until 1979, when it was sold to Pabst. Ownership passed to Heileman in 1983 and to Stroh in 1996. Bill Yenne

The consultants who guided the major brewers down this strange road pointed out that beer drinkers were more likely to be men, so in an effort to attract more women, major brewers began introducing reduced-calorie, or "light," beers in 1975. Miller's product, known simply as "Lite," or Miller Lite, was the first and today remains the world's leading reduced-calorie beer, outselling both Anheuser-Busch's Michelob Light and Bud Light.

In 1976 and 1977 the light beer phenomenon helped to fuel a 7.5 percent increase in overall beer consumption, the largest increase in the United States since World War II. By the mid-1980s, light beers had secured a permanent niche in the North American market and accounted for 22 percent of all beer being sold.

A light beer typically has between 70 and 100 calories per 12-ounce serving, compared to 150 or more for standard, mass-market lagers. This is achieved by using less malt and allowing the sugars to ferment more completely. The resulting beer is low on malt and hop flavor, but if served cold, it is "clean" and refreshing, very much to the American taste in mass-market beers. Miller also notes in its advertising that its Lite, like other lights, is "less filling."

Once the concept of a light beer was introduced, it became part of every major brewer's repertoire almost immediately. Virtually every major flagship brand in the United States and Canada marketed a companion "light" variant as well. Anheuser-Busch produced two: Bud Light to complement Budweiser, and Michelob Light for calorie-conscious Michelob

The Spoetzl Brewery of Shiner, Texas, seen here sometime in the 1970s, was typical of the small regional breweries that still survived throughout the United States at the time. Unlike most, however, Spoetzl survived the consolidation period and ended the twentieth century stronger than ever. The brewery evolved from the Shiner Brewing Association that was started in 1909, and was taken over by Betzold and Spoetzl in 1915. In 1989, Gambrinus Imports, the San Antonio-based importer of Mexico's best-selling Corona brand, purchased the company. Author's collection

devotees. Using an already recognizable brand name seemed preferable to the idea of producing an all-new product with an all-new name, such as Miller had done. Miller, after all, had been first, and had taken the most obvious new brand name. Miller Lite remained the largest selling reduced-calorie beer in the United States until 1994, when Bud Light eclipsed it for the first time.

The immense success and market acceptance of reduced-calorie beers prompted some interest among major brewers to attempt to market reduced-alcohol beers as well. Anheuser-Busch unveiled its LA (Low Alcohol) beer at the same time as the 1984 Los Angeles Olympics, of which they were a sponsor, but the phenomenal success of light beers eight years earlier was not repeated.

In the summer of 1989, Anheuser-Busch launched a third wave of new products designed to reach a wider slice of the market: Michelob Dry. By definition, a "dry beer" is a beer in which all of the fermentable sugars from the original malt are converted to alcohol. In order to conclude the process with a beer of acceptable alcohol content (roughly 3.2 percent by weight), a brewer must start with less malt. Hence, dry beer has a low original gravity and very little flavor unless it is more heavily hopped than typical beers. The process is similar to that used by brewers to produce light beer, and the results are very similar. In fact, most American mass-market lagers, including light and dry beers, are very similar in taste.

Anheuser-Busch's Michelob Dry was first, but it was quickly followed by a number of Heileman "dry" products, including Lone Star, Rainier, and Old Style. Molson, which was already producing Japan's Kirin "dry beer" under license in Canada, introduced a Molson Dry in 1989. In the early 1990s, the short-lived "dry" beer was superseded by the "ice" beer marketing phenomenon. Like "dry" beer, "ice" beer was merely a subtle variation

A beautiful stained-glass window tops the brew kettle at the Yuengling Brewery in Pottsville, Pennsylvania. The mural on the back wall includes vignettes from Yuengling's long history. Founded in 1829, it is America's oldest brewing company. Yuengling Brewing

The Lucky Lager brewery at the corner of Columbia Street and West Seventh in Vancouver, Washington, was constructed on the site of the brewery founded by John Muench in 1856 and purchased by Henry Weinhard in 1859. After a succession of owners, Lucky Lager took over the site in 1950, enlarging and expanding the brewery. For a quarter-century, the Lucky name alternated with that of the affiliated General Brewing. This picture was taken in about 1972, just before the General name was reassigned. S&P, parent of Pabst Brewing, bought the plant in 1975. In 1985, S&P completely dismantled the entire brewery and shipped it to China, where it was reassembled in Zhaoging. Author's collection

of very lightly flavored lager. Developed and patented by Labatt in Canada, it is a process by which beer is quickly chilled to sub-freezing temperatures after brewing but before final fermentation. The result is the formation of ice crystals in the beer, which are removed to produce a beer with roughly *twice* the alcohol content of typical mass-market lagers. As they had with "light" and "dry" beers, most major companies introduced an "ice" version of their major products. Neither the "dry" nor "ice" products, however, achieved the market success that "light" beers had.

Even as the major brewing companies were busily pursuing their families of less substantial beers with less taste, a grassroots revolution was brewing in the United States that would render positive changes in American brewing like the country had not seen in more than a century.

SMITHING BY
H. ZAFT
COPPER WORKS
NCISCO, CALIF.

CHAPTER

The Microbrewery Revolution

1980-1995

By 1980, the number of breweries in the United States had dwindled to fewer than 50. The Big Three owned most of the actual brewing facilities and virtually all of the brewing capacity. The small regionals rapidly dropped away or were folded into mini-conglomerates such as Heileman and Pabst.

Suddenly, the trend began to reverse. On the West Coast, *new* brewing companies began to appear. They were tiny, but they were commercially viable, and they earned strong local acceptance. They were important to the history of American brewing because they represented a new approach to regional beer and brewing. Actually, it was not "new" but, rather, reminiscent of a way of looking at beer and brewing that had not been seen in America since before Prohibition. A new breed of "craft brewer" came on the scene with the novel notion that beer should be carefully crafted rather than mass-produced. Ingredients should be selected to enhance flavor rather than to achieve "flavor neutrality" and to facilitate production and consistency.

New terms entered the lexicon. The "craft brewer" was defined as someone who looked upon brewing as an art rather than as a factory chore. They thought of themselves as chefs, rather than as factory managers. The place where this art was practiced was typically smaller than a traditional brewery, and the name "microbrewery" was adopted.

A microbrewery was originally considered to be a brewery with a capacity of less than 3,000 barrels per year, but by the end of the 1980s this threshold increased to 15,000 barrels as the demand for microbrewed beer doubled, and then tripled.

Opposite: *Brewmaster Allan Paul inspects boiling wort from the copper brew kettle at the San Francisco Brewing Company. He was in business at the same site for two decades, and he started the first brewpub in San Francisco—the city that was known as the brewing capital of the Far West in the years before Prohibition.* Bill Yenne

Fritz Maytag's Anchor Brewing Company facility on Mariposa Street in San Francisco is a mecca for beer lovers throughout the world. After Maytag saved 70-year-old Anchor from oblivion in 1965, he set a standard of craftsmanship and attention to detail that inspired a new generation of brewers, and indeed, a whole new industry. Bill Yenne

Another new entity born of the Microbrewery Revolution was the "brewpub," a microbrewery that both brewed *and* served its beer to the public on the same premises. Unlike a microbrewery, the primary market for the products of a brewpub is under its own roof. Brewpubs had existed in the United States in the eighteenth and nineteenth centuries. However, after Prohibition, it was illegal in most states and Canadian provinces to both brew beer and sell it to the public on the same premises. Changes in local laws since the early 1980s have rescinded these outdated restrictions and have made it possible for brewpubs to become widespread.

By definition, a brewpub brews to serve. Some brewpubs bottle their beers for sale to patrons and for wholesale to retailers, while some microbreweries also operate brewpubs, hence the distinction between the two can be somewhat blurred. Both, however, share a commitment to their own unique beers, and most brewpublicans enter their trade out of a love for brewing and an interest in distinctive beer styles.

Below: *The big copper brewing vessels at Anchor Brewing Company on Mariposa Street in San Francisco were built by Ziemann in Germany, and they were once installed at a small brewery in Karlsruhe. They provide Anchor with a 110-barrel daily brewing capacity.* Bill Yenne

Below: *Fritz Maytag, president of the Anchor Brewing Company in San Francisco, California, has been a leader in reviving traditional beer styles in the United States. He successfully resuscitated the Anchor Brewing Company after buying it in 1965, and he continued to serve as an inspiration for countless microbrewers in subsequent years.* Anchor Brewing Company

Above: *The copper grant at the Anchor Brewing Company was manufactured by Ziemann in Germany. After leaving the lauter tun, wort passes through the grant to be aerated and checked for clarity.* Bill Yenne

The Microbrewery Revolution gave Americans a vastly wider selection of styles and varieties of fresh, domestically produced beers than had been available since the nineteenth century. It also signaled a return to the concept of regional, and even neighborhood breweries, an idea that was thought to have perished soon after World War II.

Above: *Charles Finkel with the small copper brew kettle at the Pike Place Brewery in Seattle, circa 1991. An internationally known beer importer and promoter, Finkel started his microbrewery in the famed Pike Place Market in 1989. He has since retired from the company, now known as the Pike Brewery, which has brewed at a different Seattle location since 1996.* Bill Yenne

Right: *Dick Burke and Bruce DeRosier started Montana's first new brewery in a generation, the Kessler Brewing Company in Helena in 1982. The name was that of nineteenth-century Helena brewing legend, Nick Kessler. During its heyday in the late 1980s, the company brewed its own beer in addition to private-label beer for other companies throughout the West.* Bill Yenne

The fermenting tanks of the Hart Brewing Company in Kalama, Washington. The company began brewing its Pyramid brand ales in Kalama in 1984 and built a larger brewery in the same city in 1992. Their legendary holiday beer, Snowcap Ale, was added to the product line in 1986 and had been one of the leaders in this genre since. In 1992, Hart purchased the Thomas Kemper Brewing Company in Poulsbo, Washington. Pyramid Brewing

American brewing history was repeating itself. A new generation began to discover and take pride in local brews, just as their grandparents had. For the first time in over a century, the number of brewing companies in North America began to increase—in the United States the number of breweries went from around 40 in 1980 to 190 in 1988.

Though the Microbrewery Revolution started in 1980, a man named Fritz Maytag, who is generally credited as the inspiration for the Microbrewery Revolution and is often heralded as its patron saint, laid the foundations more than a decade earlier. Maytag would probably be the last person to wish for such a mantle, yet he is almost universally cited. Certainly, Maytag is the archetype of the "craft brewer."

In 1965, the 70-year-old Anchor Brewing in San Francisco had been on the verge of going out of business. Young Maytag, a member of the family that owns the appliance company of the same name, had enjoyed their beer during his college years and didn't want to see Anchor go away, so he bought the company. In the process, he also bought a career that would define the rest of his life, as well as the future of small-scale brewing in the United States. At a time when many brewing companies were cutting corners with such tactics as substituting corn and rice for

The alehouse at the Pyramid Brewing Company in Seattle. In 1995, Hart Brewing of Kalama constructed its Seattle brewery, and the following year it was renamed in honor of its Pyramid Ales brand name. A few years later, the Seattle Mariners constructed their new stadium across the street from the Pyramid alehouse. The company that started in a small logging town's general store is now listed on the NASDAQ. Pyramid Brewing

They say that location is everything, and the late Times Square Brewery Restaurant certainly had a prime location. Unfortunately, New York City has not proven to be a good location for brewpubs, as evidenced by the demise of a number of well-known names, from Chelsea Brewing to Manhattan Brewing to Zip City. For several of the brewpubs, it was not so much the location that sounded the death knell, but the quality of the beer—and for a brewpub, that is everything. Bill Yenne

barley, Maytag threw himself into maintaining and nurturing the highest quality beer possible.

During his first two decades, Maytag increased Anchor's output 75-fold. The company's flagship product is Anchor Steam Beer, which has become one of America's most prized premium beers. It was developed by master brewer Maytag himself, and is loosely based on what is known of the legendary "steam" beers produced in gold rush days. Other Anchor products include Anchor Porter, Anchor Liberty Ale, and Old Foghorn Barley Wine–style Ale, which was first produced in 1975. Anchor is also renowned locally for its annual Christmas beer, which has been specially brewed since 1975, with a different recipe each year.

As Maytag was working to transform Anchor, the first actual microbrewery to start from scratch was taking shape about 90 minutes north of San Francisco. New Albion Brewing, founded in 1976 by Jack McAuliffe in Sonoma, California, was the first microbrewery. Though New Albion would not survive the decade, McAuliffe's experiment served as the prototype for a new generation of microbreweries.

After New Albion, it was several years before the Microbrewery Revolution began to spread. In 1980, River City Brewing opened in Sacramento, California, and Sierra Nevada Brewing opened in nearby Chico. While River City survived only a few years, Sierra Nevada is now one of the largest brewing companies in North America.

The microbrewery movement spread to Colorado in 1980 with the opening of the Boulder

F.X. Matt II was the president of the Matt (a.k.a. West End) Brewing Company in Utica, New York, from 1980 until his death in 2001. Unlike many of his contemporaries, Matt embraced the craft-brewing trend and revamped the family brewery with contract brewing and specialty brands. Fully engaged in this renaissance, he was a hands-on manager, striding through the brewery each and every morning, carrying a small memorandum book, and jotting down frequent notes as he talked to his brewers and production people. Matt Brewing via author's collection

Dock Street Brewing was founded in 1986 by Philadelphia chef Jeffrey Ware. The beer was contract-brewed until Ware opened his Dock Street Brewery & Restaurant on Logan Square in 1990—notice the brew kettles in the background. During the 1990s he also briefly operated the Dock Street Brewing Company restaurant in Washington, D.C. Dock Street Brewing

Far right: *Jim Koch's family had been involved in American brewing since the establishment of the Fred Koch Brewery of Dunkirk, New York, in 1888. Anxious to be back in the family business, Koch started the Boston Beer Company in 1985 to produce Samuel Adams Lager, an American craft beer named for the eighteenth-century Boston patriot and maltster. By the year 2000, Koch's company was the largest of the wave of new breweries started after 1980.* Boston Beer Company

Brewing Company (Rockies Brewing since 1993), and to New York State when William Newman began brewing in Albany the following year. Two important microbreweries also opened in Washington State during 1982: Paul Shipman's Red Hook Ale Brewery in Seattle and Bert Grant's Yakima Brewing & Malting, which is coincidentally located in the heart of the best hop-growing region in North America.

Certainly one aspect of the Microbrewery Revolution that cannot be overemphasized is that of the introduction—or reintroduction—of a variety of specialty beer styles. By 1980, most American consumers had come to think of the term "beer" as synonymous with the watery, light-yellow stuff sold by the megabrewers. There was a reason that beer was reduced to this definition. The megabrewers operated many large-volume brewing plants in far-flung locations, and it was vital to maintain consistency in their product. Homogeneity in flavor is, of course, best achieved by reducing the complexity of the product and reducing the number of ingredients that affect the flavor.

With the Microbrewery Revolution, beer lovers suddenly had unfettered access to rich amber ale, opaque stouts, and true pilsen-style lagers. These beers were made the way that they actually made them in Pilsen. Making beers that were "flavor neutral" was the last thing the craft brewers wanted to accomplish.

Beer styles that most Americans had never heard of suddenly became available. In Modesto, California, Stanislaus Brewing introduced St. Stan's Altbier, a style that then existed in and around Dusseldorf, Germany, but nowhere else. Fruit beers found in Belgium and virtually nowhere else until after 1980 cropped up at craft brewing operations in the United States from Oregon to Wisconsin.

One case study in the pioneering of new American beer styles centers on the Oregon coastal city of Newport, with an entrepreneur named Jack Joyce, and a brewer named John Maier. Joyce came into the world of brewing in 1988 as a refugee from the corporate rat race with the idea of investing in the Rogue Brewery & Public House in Ashland, Oregon, but he soon found himself running the place. The idea of building a second establishment of that kind came about by accident when he happened to be stranded in Newport for four days in February 1989. Many people thought that Newport was right for a

Above: *A member of the Sierra Nevada staff at the company's Chico, California, brewery inspects some hops of the Hallertau variety that were grown in Yakima County, Washington, in 1988.* Inset: *First brewed in 1980, Sierra Nevada Pale Ale was one of the original microbrews. Hence the name, this beer was brewed in the foothills of the Sierra Nevada moutain range. By the turn of the twenty-first century, it had emerged as the largest-selling microbrewed beer in America.* Sierra Nevada Brewing

brewpub, and not the least of these was the family of Mo Niemi, who had owned and operated a half dozen family-style seafood cafés on the Oregon coast for the better part of half a century. The result was the Bayfront Brewery, a brewpub and soon the primary brewing operation of Joyce's product line of Rogue Ales. Joyce hired John Maier as brewmaster.

Maier had started brewing in Southern California in the early 1980s, earned the title of American Homebrewers Association (AHA) Homebrewer of the Year in 1988, and was hired by Chinook Alaskan Brewing (now Alaskan Brewing) in Juneau. In Alaska, Maier gained national attention for brewing what may have been the first American smoked beer—a beer made with malt that was toasted over a smoky wood fire in a manner reminiscent of Germany's Bamberger *rauchbiers*. When Jack Joyce hired him for the Newport brewery, John Maier

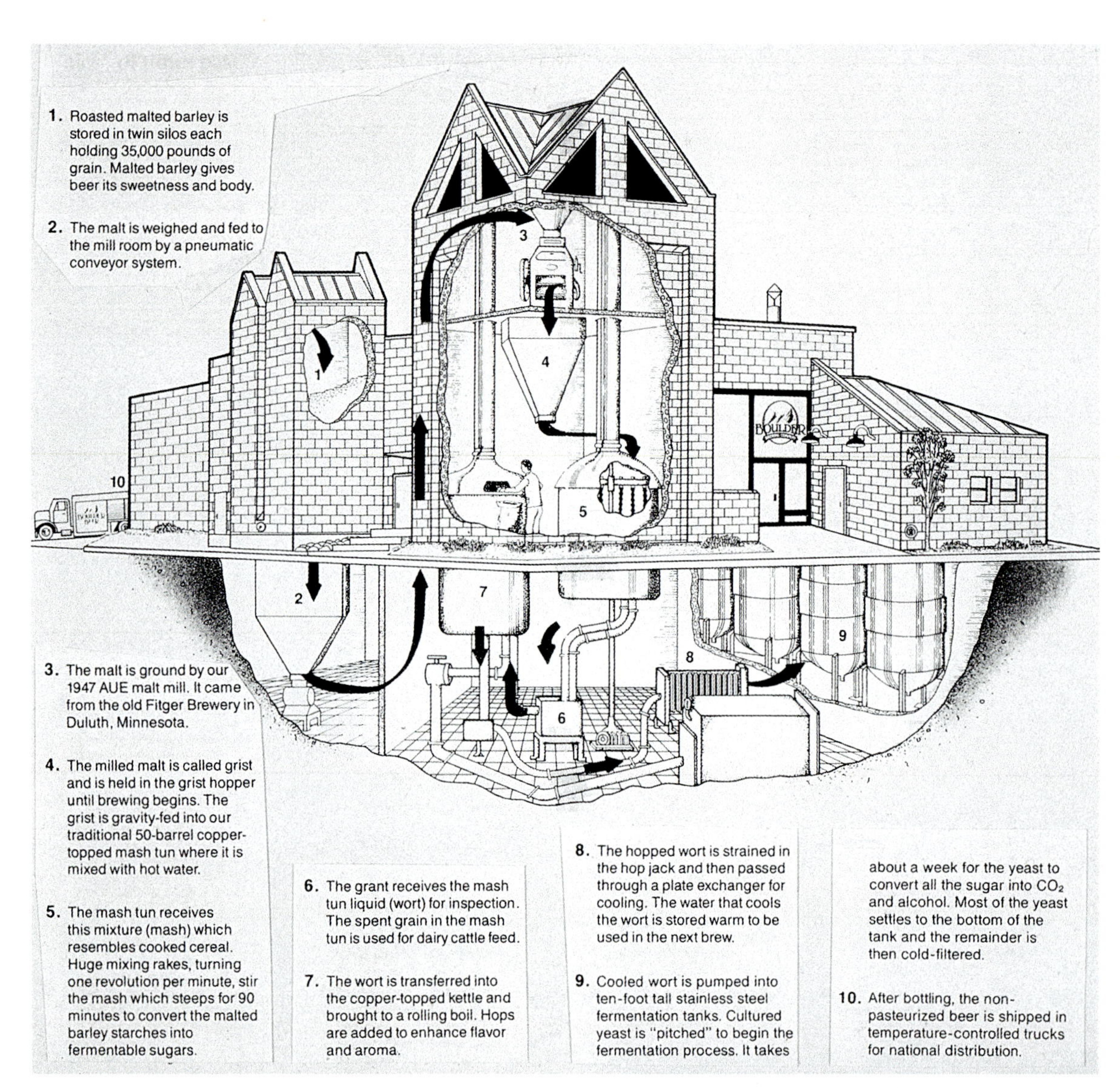

Known as the Rockies Brewing Company since 1993, Colorado's first microbrewery was founded in 1979 as Boulder Brewing Company by David Hummer and Stick Ware. This cutaway illustration of the brewery (drawn when the company was still known as Boulder Brewing) clearly shows the brewing process within a turn-of-the-century microbrewery. The process begins with malted barley that proceeds to the brew kettle by way of the mash tun. The barley then brews into the wort, which ferments into beer.
Boulder Brewing

created a smoked beer called Rogue Welkommen that would win a gold medal at the 1990 Great American Beer Festival.

The Rogue Brewery & Public House in Ashland was eventually closed, and in 1991, Rogue moved its brewing operations across the Yaquina River from the Bayfront pub, which remained in operation. In 1998, Rogue bought a 50-barrel brew system for the new brewery. At the turn of the century, Maier was still brewing his smoked beer, now known simply as Rogue Smoke Ale.

Of course, microbreweries were not the only institutions to benefit from Fritz Maytag's bold experiment. The public's heightened awareness of distinctive specialty beers created an expanded market for other small, regional brewers whose existence predated the Microbrewery Revolution. A good example was August Schell Brewing of New Ulm, Minnesota. Founded in 1860, the company endured early growing pains that might have sounded its death knell—the brewery survived the 1862 Sioux Uprising because of August Schell's excellent rapport with the tribe. For 125 years, Schell weathered the ups and downs of the market as a traditional regional brewery, but the Microbrewery Revolution led to the company's "rediscovery." In 1988, the Great American Beer Festival called August Schell Pilsner "unquestionably America's finest Pilsner beer."

In 1982, Bert Grant opened America's first brewpub in more than a century, and others soon followed. Mendocino Brewing, which was established in the appropriately named village of Hopland, about two hours north of San Francisco, opened in 1983 and was followed by Buffalo Bill Owens' brewpub in Hayward, across the Bay from San Francisco.

By the time that Allen Paul opened San Francisco Brewing in the old Albatross Saloon in 1986, there was a rush of new brewpubs opening throughout the United States. Mike and Brian McMenamin led the revolution into the Northwest in 1985 with the Hillsdale in Portland, and within four years they had opened six brewpubs in western Oregon.

The first generation of American brewpubs set a benchmark for general ambiance that is still common today. Brewpubs are generally small, comfortable, informal venues, with the look and feel of traditional neighborhood bars. They are usually decorated with local historical ephemera or beer memorabilia. If food is served, it usually consists of sandwiches, burgers, and snacks. The overall emphasis of brewpubs is on their *raison d'etre*—beer.

The original Gordon Biersch brewhouse in Palo Alto, California. The idea, as used by many brewpub operators, was to permit bar patrons to actually watch the brewing process. Gordon Biersch

A view of the main restaurant seating area and part of the kitchen area at the original Gordon Biersch brewery/restaurant. Dan Gordon and Dean Biersch began operations in 1988 at this facility on Emerson Street in Palo Alto.
Gordon Biersch

Born in 1928 in Dundee, Scotland, Bert Grant (left) worked as a brewer in the United States and Canada before opening America's first brewpub in Yakima, Washington, in 1983. He went on to bottle his products, incurring the wrath of the United States government by printing nutritional information (expressly forbidden by law) on his labels. Grant retired in 1994 and sold his company to Stimson Lane. After a long illness, he died in July 2001.
Yakima Brewing & Malting

Everything else, the theme and the feel of the place, is designed to support and enhance that central feature.

As with contemporary microbreweries, brewpub brewers quickly adopted the idea of providing a range of beer styles that was as broad as possible. The standard bar of the 1980s offered only one style of beer, as many as a dozen brands of thin, light-yellow lager, including imported light-yellow lager, and even "light" versions of well-known light-yellow lagers. Brewpub owners became zealots in a crusade to offer their patrons a choice.

Because they brewed in smaller quantities than microbreweries, brewpubs could offer an even wider range of products ranging from the strange to the truly sublime. The mere fact that they were offered was the real point of the story. The typical brewpub of the 1980s offered between a half-dozen and a dozen choices that were more widely varied than nearly any American bar patron

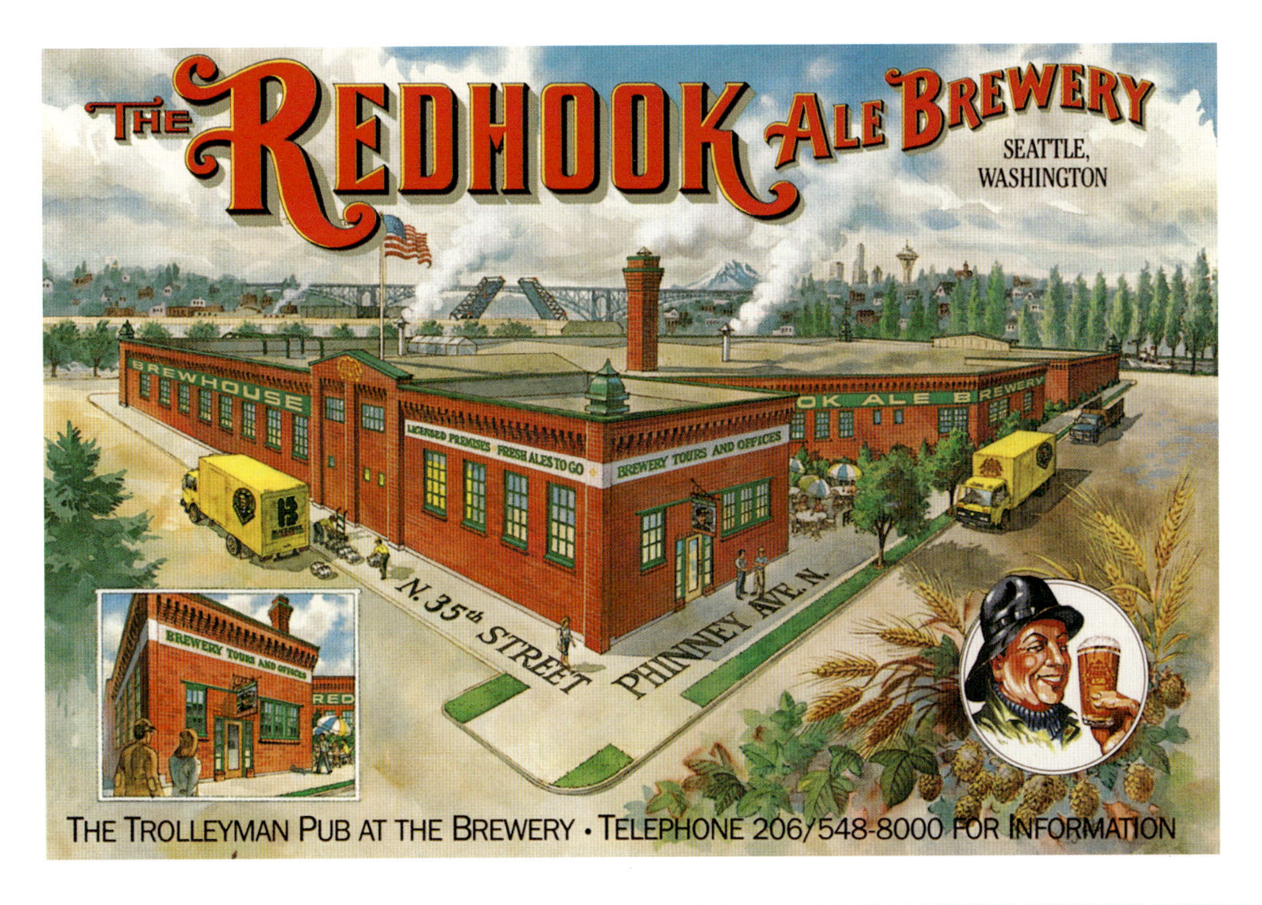

This well-known Redhook Ale Brewery advertising piece was created by using artwork that was similar in style to illustrations of redbrick industrial buildings from the nineteenth century. The idea behind the advertisement was to show factories, including breweries, from elevated and panoramic perspectives. Such renderings showed the factories in the context of the neighborhoods that they occupied, with factory workers busily going about their tasks. Redhook

Pictured in this 1989 photograph are the three founders of Boston's Mass Bay Brewing Company. Rich Doyle, George Ligeti, and Dan Kenary (from left to right) started the company in 1986 and delivered the first beer from their Harpoon Brewery on Northern Avenue in Boston in June 1987. Mass Bay Brewing Company

had ever seen. The flagship beer was usually an amber ale, and most first-generation brewpubs offered both a porter and a stout. There was also usually a beer that was lighter than the flagship amber, and a couple of specialty beers. These might include a seasonal specialty or the results of a brewmaster's particular brainstorm.

Today's brewpubs still offer a broad range of colors and flavors. A "sampler," a set of small glasses of all the establishment's beers is usually offered. Viewing this sampler is usually instructive of the variety available. The colors will range from nearly opaque black to a yellow that is nearly as pale as a mass-market lager.

At the opposite end of the brewpub spectrum from the small, neighborhood tavern was the Oldenberg Brewery that operated from 1988 to 1999 in Fort Mitchell, Kentucky, across the Ohio River from Cincinnati. With about fifty times the square footage of most typically modest brewpubs, Oldenberg was a beer drinkers' amusement park.

Mass Bay Brewing Company staff serves Harpoon Ale and Harpoon Golden Lager to the happy attendees of a Boston beer festival in May 1993. Many brewing companies make appearances at major beer festivals such as this one because the festivals serve as a vital form of advertising. Mass Bay Brewing Company

The centerpiece was an immense beer hall that seated 650 people, had a 65-foot ceiling, and offered live entertainment. There was also a smaller brewpub and an outdoor beer garden.

By the 1990s, the brewpub scene had matured considerably. While the archetypal brewpubs continued to flourish, the definition of brewpub had been stretched to include full-service restaurants that brewed beer. This trend was indicative of the fact that beer is just as valid a complement to fine cuisine as wine. This recognition evolved as a result of the wide variety of beer styles that had become available, each one with a particular character that complements a particular type of food.

The Gordon Biersch chain, which was born in Palo Alto, California, in 1988, is a good example of the genre of full-service restaurants that also brew beer. The concept was created by a partnership between a brewer, Dan Gordon, and a chef, Dean Biersch. By the mid-1990s, Gordon and Biersch had locations in three northern California cities, and by the turn of the century the company that they had founded was serving patrons in a dozen locations across the United States.

Another brewing industry phenomenon that came to the fore in the late 1980s and early 1990s was that of "contract brewing." Under contract brewing, Brewing Company A has a brand and a label—Brand A—but no brewery. The beer is actually produced by Company B and labeled with the Brand A. Company B may also produce its own Brand B beer, as well as Brand C and Brand D products for other "brewing companies" that don't have breweries. Contract brewing allows many entrepreneurs with ideas for products to get them on the shelf without having to construct breweries.

While the Microbrewery Revolution was born in the West, where actually having a brewery was considered to be a prerequisite for having a brewing company, contract brewing first emerged in the major markets of the Northeast. Philadelphia, New York, and Boston each saw the development of a major local brand that was actually brewed under contract somewhere else.

Far left: *Santa Fe Brewing Company founder and brewmaster Mike Levis at his original ranch brewery in February 1990. Levis was a horse rancher and part-owner of a packaging company in Phoenix, Arizona, when he first started thinking about brewing in the mid-1980s. In 1987, he started the Santa Fe Brewing Company at his Flying M Ranch. The ranch was located at the end of a dirt road that winds through the piñon-studded foothills about a mile north of the nearby village of Galisteo. He would continue brewing on the ranch until 1996, when he sold the company to his son Ty, who moved operations into Santa Fe.* Bill Yenne

Left: *Brewmaster John Maier (right) with brewery owner Jack Joyce in the Rogue Ales fermentation room adjacent to the Bayfront Brewery in Newport, Oregon, in June 1991. A former award-winning home brewer, Maier came to Rogue from Chinook Alaskan Brewing in Juneau, Alaska. Joyce hired Maier after the latter made a name for himself in the industry by becoming the first American brewmaster in memory to use smoked malt in his beers. The late Chuck Linquist, who described himself as a factotum, volunteered to smoke the malt for Maier's beer. Chuck had never smoked malt before, but he had smoked meat and fish. He got some cherry wood, took a bag of Crystal Malt home, and soon Rogue smoked beer was a reality.* Bill Yenne

Contract brewing was not, however, confined to any one region. Montana Beverages of Helena, a microbrewery founded in 1982, did not only brew its own Kessler brand, it also produced products for brewing companies throughout the West.

One of the first and best-known entrepreneurs to use contract brewing was Jim Koch of Boston, who formed his Boston Beer Company in 1985 to produce Samuel Adams Lager. His idea was to create an American beer—named for the eighteenth-century Boston patriot and maltster—that could compete with the best German beers and pass the Reinheitsgebot (German Purity Law). "Sam Adams" passed the test and was actually sold in West Germany before Koch expanded his marketing in the United States beyond the Boston area. By the early 1990s, Sam Adams was available throughout the United States.

Both of Philadelphia's initial "house" brands—Jeff Ware's Dock Street and Tom Pastorius's Pennsylvania Pilsner—were originally contract brewed, but Pastorius opened his own brewery in Pittsburgh in 1989. Two other early contract brewing companies in leading eastern markets were the Brooklyn Brewery, founded in 1988, and Olde Heurich Brewing in Washington, D.C., founded by Gary Heurich, grandson of Christian Heurich, who built his brewery in 1873 on the site where the Kennedy Center now stands.

In New York City, the first new brewing companies in town after the Microbrewery Revolution began were Old New York, whose Amsterdam Amber was brewed under contract by F.X. Matt Brewing in Utica, New York, and Manhattan Brewing, a brewpub. Robert D'Addona started the now defunct Manhattan Brewing in 1984 in a former Consolidated Edison substation on Thompson Street in the city's SoHo district.

F.X. Matt—a.k.a. West End Brewing Company—evolved into one of the largest of the contract brewers in the East during the late 1980s and early 1990s. Originally founded in 1853, the company that had long been famous for its own Utica Club

In addition to the nineteenth-century retro styling of its buildings, the Oldenberg Brewery also operated a vintage 1920s beer truck. Although the truck was used for deliveries, its predominant function was for promotional appearances, including trips across the Ohio River into Cincinnati, which was once the brewing capital of the entire region. Bill Yenne

brand contracted brew for a number of eastern companies during the 1980s and 1990s. In its heyday, the brewery produced over 600,000 barrels per annum of the Utica Club and Matt's Premium flagship beers but, like many smaller brewing companies, it had suffered a gradual decline of these traditional brands in the 1970s and 1980s. For Matt, the specialty beer wave arrived in the nick of time. F.X. Matt II, who took the helm of the family business in 1980, reinvented the company, replacing declining brands with contract brewing and with the best-selling Saranac specialty line.

Just as contract brewing was not confined to the East, all of the new brewers in the East were not contract brewers. William Newman led the way in Albany, and Robert D'Addona followed in Manhattan. Among the first outside the Empire State were D.L. Geary Brewing in Portland, Maine, and Catamount Brewing in White River Junction, Vermont, which opened in 1986 and 1987, respectively. Another early eastern micro was Mass Bay Brewing—famous for the Harpoon brand—which began brewing in Boston in 1987, and which was among the top ten specialty brewers in the United States at the turn of the century.

The proliferation of new breweries changed the face of American brewing. With an increase from around 40 in 1980 to 190 in 1988, the number of

Above: *The Oldenberg Brewery and "entertainment complex" on Buttermilk Pike in Ft Mitchell, Kentucky, opened in 1988 and remained in business during most of the 1990s. In addition to the brewery and the "J.D. Brew's" pub, the complex contained a vast beer hall. In terms of customer floor space, it was probably the largest "brewpub" of its era.* Inset: *The weather vane atop the Oldenberg Brewery's huge beer hall featured a beer keg. The Oldenberg complex was deliberately constructed to resemble nineteenth-century brewery buildings, complete with the most intricate architectural detailing. This cupola was atop the beer hall's 65-foot ceiling.* Bill Yenne

American breweries reached 500 by 1995, the highest since World War II. By 1996, there were more breweries in the United States than in Germany, yet another major milestone.

In an interview in *Modern Brewery Age*, William Coors recalled that in 1965 he told Henry King, head of the United States Brewers' Association, that "if the industry continued the way it was going, by the millennium we would be down to five breweries. I was simply extrapolating the death curve out. I didn't take into account this eruption of pub and boutique breweries. I think it's the best thing that has happened to the brewing industry, if you really want to know . . . it definitely adds to the cultural acceptance of beer."

This comfortable bar area is at the North Coast Brewing brewpub in Fort Bragg on California's Mendocino County coast. The brewery began operations in 1988 under the leadership of brewmaster Mark Ruedrich and his associates, Joe Rosenthal and Tom Allen. Situated in an old nineteenth-century mortuary, the brewery originally had an annual capacity of 700 barrels. By the turn of the twenty-first century, a bottle line had been added, and as Red Seal Ale became widely popular, annual production increased twentyfold. North Coast Brewing

The American Brewery in the Twenty-first Century

Even for someone who had slept through the twentieth century, the status of the American brewing industry at the end of that century would have held a few surprises . . . but only a few. Prohibition had come and gone, but left no perceptible trace. The dramatic decline in the number of breweries in the United States, which had occurred between 1950 and 1980, had been reversed, so that there were 1,500 breweries in 2000, about the same number as there had been in 1900.

A Rip van Winkle–like beer drinker from 1900 would have actually suffered more culture shock awakening in 1975 than in 2000. But after the dismal situation of the 1970s, things had rebounded. By 2000, many towns and neighborhoods that had proudly boasted a local brewery in 1900 had a brewery again. And, as in 1900, the beer was made with barley again, rather than with corn and rice.

In terms of the big names in the industry, our nineteenth-century time-traveler would find them familiar. Pabst, the biggest name at the beginning of the twentieth century had faded to near obscurity during the century only to surge back to the number four position as the century ended. The top two in 2000, Anheuser-Busch and Miller, had both been in the top ten a century earlier. At number three, Coors had been a smaller regional in 1900, but it was not unknown.

After their heralded rise to prominence, Stroh and Heileman had moved into the top five and were enjoying solid growth. Between them, they controlled 40 percent of the United States market in the 1980s. In 1996, the two came together, but by the beginning of the twenty-first century, they were both gone. But the time-traveler from 1900 would not have noticed—both had been just small regionals in 1900.

Opposite: *The brewhouse at the Spoetzl Brewery in Shiner, Texas. Dating back to the original Shiner Brewing Association that was formed in 1909, Spoetzl evolved steadily through the twentieth century, maintaining a strong local following while bigger brands came and went.* Spoetzl Brewery

The legendary Hopland Brewery on the main street of Hopland, California, is a landmark of American brewing history. In August 1983, Mendocino Brewing Company opened it as the first brewpub in California since Prohibition and the second brewpub in the United States. Commercial bottling began soon after, and demand for their Red Tail Ale soon made it one of the most popular microbrews in the West. Now brewing and bottling at a state-of-the-art brewery in nearby Ukiah, Mendocino Brewing in 2003 was the third largest California-based brewery. The Hopland Brewery remains as both a historic icon and a good place to take a break while out for a bike ride. Bill Yenne

Bayern Brewing was founded in Missoula, Montana, in 1987 by brewmaster Jürgen Knoller as a German-style brewpub. The original brewpub closed, but Bayern continues to operate as a Missoula microbrewery, serving the Iron Horse pub in Missoula and this "brewpub" in Butte. Bill Yenne

He would, however, find it curiously ironic that the Schlitz name—Pabst's greatest rival in 1900—was now owned by the same holding company as Pabst!

But of all the changes wrought on American brewing in the twentieth century, perhaps the most remarkable is the fact that of the top 200 breweries in the United States at the turn of the twenty-first century, all were founded either *before 1910* or *after 1980*. In retrospect, it may seem surprising how some of the major trends of the 1980s have played out. During the 1980s, and even into the early 1990s, many outside the industry labeled microbreweries as a fad and predicted their imminent demise. Far from this, the microbreweries were the fastest-growing segment of the market as the century turned.

In 1999, the industry experienced what some analysts referred to as "the final consolidation." The phrase was obviously eve-of-the-millennium hyperbole, but clearly the implosion of Stroh (which had absorbed Heileman in 1996), whose tumbling dominos affected both Miller and Pabst, was the biggest news to hit the top end of the industry since the 1970s.The big three at the turn of the century were the big three of 1990. Anheuser-Busch was in

Above: *In 1987, the Full Sail Brewing Company began operations at this facility in Hood River, Oregon, overlooking the Columbia River. The name is derived from Hood River's prominence as the windsurfing capital of the Columbia River Gorge. Employee-owned since 1999, Full Sail has outgrown its microbrewery status and is now the third largest brewery based in Oregon, a state that is known as a leading center of craft brewing.* Bill Yenne

Bottom left: *Full Sail's signature product is its Amber Ale, brewed with two-row pale, crystal, and chocolate malts and hopped with Mount Hood and Cascade hops. Full Sail is arguably the closest major brewery to the most important hop-growing region in the United States. By the turn of the century, the brewing of rich, distinctive, spiced December holiday beers had become a tradition with many major craft brewers.* Bottom right: *One of the most successful was Full Sail's Wassail, which is brewed with four types of malts and is hopped with a special blend of imported hops. The term* wassail *refers to the centuries-old English tradition of such holiday ales. At least as far back as the eighteenth century, people who went house-to-house singing Christmas carols carried a bowl and were rewarded at each house with a splash of homemade wassail, a spiced ale or wine.* Full Sail Brewing Company

the lead, with Miller Brewing in second and Coors in third place. During a decade when overall American beer consumption had remained essentially flat, as it were, both Anheuser-Busch and Coors had posted modest increases of 13.6 and 19.8 percent, respectively. Miller, meanwhile, declined by 4.4 percent in the 1990s.

Certainly, Anheuser-Busch grew so robustly that it is clearly the twentieth-century success story in United States brewing. It is the largest brewing company in the United States and the world, but it is more than that. Still reflecting the expansive 1876 vision of Adolphus Busch, today the company is a well-integrated corporation with a diversification that ranges from theme parks to major-league sports. Anheuser-Busch is an unrivaled industry leader that is larger than the rest of the industry in the United States combined.

At the beginning of the twentieth century, the industry buzzed about million-barrel brewers. A century later, Anheuser-Busch was the world's first *hundred million* barrel brewer, with sales of 98 million in the United States and 105 million barrels worldwide. The Anheuser-Busch domestic market share, which stood at 28 percent in 1980, crept past the halfway point during the 1990s to stand at 53 percent in 2000. Anheuser-Busch had accomplished the increase in market share the old-fashioned way: by increasing its volume from 50 million barrels in 1980 to 80 million in 1990.

Miller, meanwhile, had spent the 1990s rediscovering itself and introducing new brands. Plank Road, the original name of the brewery that Fred Miller bought from the Best Brothers in 1853, had been revived briefly in the mid-1980s as a Miller brand. A decade later, in 1994, the name resurfaced as Miller's "Plank Road Brewery," under which the giant began brewing their Red Dog and Icehouse brands. In 1997 and 1998, Miller revived

The BridgePort brewery and brewpub in the historic Pearl District of Portland, Oregon. The company was started in 1984 as the Columbia River Brewery by wine-makers Dick and Nancy Ponzi and brewmaster Karl Ockert. It was purchased in 1995 by the San Antonio–based Gambrinus Company, the beer importer that owns Spoetzl Brewing. BridgePort is now the fourth largest brewing company in Oregon. Bill Yenne

Above: *Kurt and Rob Widmer, who had the idea of creating American interpretations of European beer styles, started the largest brewing company in Oregon, Widmer Brothers Brewing Company, in 1984.* Left: *The Widmer brothers pioneered hefeweizen—golden, unfiltered wheat beer—in the United States in 1986. Their product has since earned the Gold Medal at the Great American Beer Festival and become their most successful brand.* Widmer Brothers Brewing

its decades-old "Miller Time" advertising slogan and brought back the long-abandoned "Girl-in-the-Moon" logo that had originated in the nineteenth century. On the business side, Miller bought, then sold, a 20 percent stake in Molson Breweries of Canada between 1993 and 1997.

No discussion of Miller Brewing and its late–twentieth-century acquisitions is complete without mention of the Jacob Leinenkugel Brewing Company of Chippewa Falls, Wisconsin. Dating back to 1867, the

Above: *While Portland, Oregon, was earning a reputation as the craft-brewing capital of the West, a similar distinction was being earned in the East by Portland, Maine. The first stop for beer lovers visiting the city, Gritty McDuff's opened in 1988 as the first brewpub in Maine since Prohibition. While brewing products such as Sebago Light and Portland Headlight Pale Ale, the pub went on to become an institution and an icon in the craft brew movement in Maine and the Northeast. Gritty's original brewhouse was designed and manufactured in 1988 by Peter Austin of Ringwood, Hampshire, England.* Bill Yenne

company was a strong regional brand that was purchased by Miller Brewing in 1987. It was never incorporated into Miller as a subsidiary, but was held autonomously as a separate operating unit. Ironically, as Miller's sales declined 4.4 percent in the 1990s, those of Leinenkugel, reported separately from Miller, *increased* by 4.3 percent. Listed separately from Miller, Leinenkugel was the eleventh largest brewing company in the United States at the turn of the century. In addition to the original Chippewa Falls facility, Leinenkuegel is brewed at the Milwaukee microbrewery built by Heileman in 1986 to showcase their revival of the Val Blatz brand as a specialty beer.

For the company that Fred Miller had bought from the Best Brothers in 1853, the biggest news a century and a half later, however, was another change of ownership. In 2002, after 33 years in the portfolio of tobacco giant Philip Morris, Miller was sold to a brewing company. On May 30, 2002, it was announced that London-based South African Breweries (SAB) had agreed to buy Miller from Philip Morris for $5.6 billion. The acquisition created the world's second-largest brewing behind Anheuser-Busch, knocking Heineken out of second place for the first time in decades. The name of this new entity would be SABMiller.

By the time of the Miller merger, SAB had become the world's fourth largest brewing company in the same manner that Heileman had become the fifth largest American brewer in the 1980s: through acquisition. SAB, known in Africa for its well-established Castle brand, is a consortium formed in 1895. It worked its way into a place as the largest brewing company in Africa during the mid-twentieth century and entered the world market through the acquisitions of companies such as Pilsner

In 1994, Minott Wessinger, the great-great-grandson of Henry Weinhard, started a brewery in Whitefish, Montana, to brew his Black Star lager. Family friend and world-renowned architect Joe Escherick designed this unique building and the Great Northern Brewing Company was born. Other products added to the line include a lager flavored with wild huckleberries. In 2002, Wessinger left the company, which is now owned by longtime Great Northern brewers Keven Guercio and Dan Rasmussen. Bill Yenne

Urquell in the Czech Republic. By the 1990s, SAB was also the largest non-Chinese brewer in China.

Another foreign-owned American brewing company that was among the top ten in the United States throughout the 1990s was Latrobe Brewing, located in the Pennsylvania town of the same name. It was established in 1893 at a time when the town's only other brewery was located at St. Vincent's Abbey and operated by Benedictine monks. The brewery at St. Vincent's closed in 1898 after 42 years of operation, but the brewery that took the name of the town survived. The flagship Rolling Rock brand is named for the nearby Rolling Rock Estate, a horse ranch. An intriguing detail about Rolling Rock is the presence of the mysterious "33" symbol that appears on the back of the bottle. Apparently, no one at the company itself can remember why it was put there in the first place because the product was introduced in 1939. Numerous contests have been held through the years to come up with clever solutions to the conundrum.

In 1987, Labatt Breweries, Canada's largest brewing company, acquired Latrobe Brewing. In 1995, Labatt was, in turn, acquired by Belgium-based Interbrew, one of the world's largest brewery holding companies, with operations spanning Europe and the Asia-Pacific region.

The largest brewpub chain in New York City at the turn of the twenty-first century, the Heartland Brewery defied the notion that brewpubs cannot survive in the Big Apple. The original location on Union Square (seen here) opened in 1995 with Jim Migliorini as brewmaster. In 1998, a second location opened in Midtown near Radio City; in 2001, other locations were added at Times Square and the South Street Seaport. Bill Yenne

During the 1990s, Latrobe, like Pabst, posted sales increases that were more than triple those of Anheuser-Busch and Coors. Latrobe was up 60.8 percent, while Pabst rose 66.7 percent. This was not bad in a flat market, and it was especially significant for Pabst, a company that many analysts would have put on the "death watch" list in the 1980s.

Both Pabst and Miller were also players in the massive industry shuffle that occurred in the late 1990s. It affected four of the greatest names in American brewing history, and four names that had been familiar on the top ten lists for half a century.

The copper brew kettles are displayed proudly at the Sierra Nevada Brewery in Chico, California. This facility is the largest former microbrewery in the United States. After expanding operations and posting growth of more than 1,500 percent during the 1990s, Sierra Nevada was brewing a half-million barrels annually at this location by the time the twenty-first century rolled around. Sierra Nevada Brewing

Left: *The snow-covered entrance to the Public House at the Deschutes Brewery in Bend, Oregon. The brewery is well known throughout the West for its gold-medal-winning Black Butte Porter. By the turn of the century, Deschutes was the second largest brewing company in Oregon, with an annual output exceeding 100,000 barrels.* Deschutes Brewing

The so-called "final consolidation" of 1999 centered on the implosion of Stroh and its Heileman brands, but both Miller and Pabst played important roles, as well.

In the summer of 1996, Stroh had acquired Heileman's five breweries, including the main Heileman plant in La Crosse, Wisconsin; Weinhard in Portland; and Rainier in Seattle; along with the Heileman brands, such as Special Export, Old Style, Rainier, Henry Weinhard, and Lone Star. Previously, Heileman had bought the Grain Belt brand of Minneapolis and later acquired Jacob Schmidt Brewing from across the river in St. Paul. In 1991, Heileman sold the Grain Belt name and Schmidt's St. Paul brewery to the Minnesota Brewing Company. By this time, Stroh had closed its own Detroit flagship brewery and was operating mainly through the 1982 acquisition of Schlitz. These included the plants at Winston-Salem, North Carolina, and Tampa, Florida.

Within a few years of swallowing Heileman in 1996, however, the caché of Stroh's large brand portfolio had faded somewhat. By that time, a major part of the company's business was contract brewing for companies such as old rival Pabst and that new upstart, Boston Beer Company, purveyors of the fast-growing Samuel Adams brand. In 1999, when Jim Koch of Boston Beer decided to pull out of Stroh and move to Miller, John Stroh III announced that the Stroh family would pull the plug on the family business a year short of its 150th birthday.

The Stroh family, in turn, sold its Stroh's and Heileman brands to Miller and Pabst. Most went to Pabst, although Miller acquired the Henry Weinhard and Blitz-Weinhard brands, along with the magnificent old Weinhard brewery building in downtown Portland. The brands were retained, but the building was recycled as an office building. The historic last brew was bottled on August 26, 1999.

The owners of the Odell Brewing Company celebrate the anniversary of their 90 Schilling (a product named for a Scottish tax based on a beer's alcohol content). From left, they are Wynne Odell; her husband, Doug; and Doug's sister, Corkie. In 1989, Odell began operations in Fort Collins as Colorado's second microbrewery. By 2000, the company was selling 21,000 barrels annually across eight states. Odell Brewing

From Pabst, Miller also took control of the venerable Hamm's brand, and with it, the legendary former Olympia brewery in Tumwater, Washington. Hamm's had bought Olympia in 1983, and had been acquired by Pabst parent S&P in 1985. Miller announced in October 1999 that it intended to invest $10 million to modernize and increase the production capacity at Tumwater. While Miller assumed control of the brewery, the Olympia brand remained part of the Pabst portfolio.

After shedding Hamm's and letting Miller take the Weinhard name, Pabst acquired the rest of the surviving former Heileman and Stroh brand names. The "Heileman" name was retained in the case of the company's former flagship brands, which were still called Heileman's Old Style and Heileman's Special Export.

Other familiar regional brands that Heileman had collected remained officially alive, although they were no longer brewed in the regions that had made them significant. They included such household names as Blatz, Falstaff, Heidelberg, Lucky Lager,

THE TOP TEN U.S. BREWING COMPANIES AT THE TURN OF THE TWENTY-FIRST CENTURY

Company and Rank*	2000 Annual Output (Millions of Barrels)	1990 Annual Output (Millions of Barrels)	Percentage change**
1. (1) Anheuser-Busch	98.3	86.5	13.6
2. (2) Miller	41.6	43.5	-4.4
3. (3) Coors	23.0	19.2	19.8
4. (6) Pabst	10.5	6.36	6.7
5. (7) Genesee	1.4	2.2	-38.6
6. (15) Boston Beer	1.2	0.1	1008
7. (9) Latrobe	1.2	0.7	60.8
8. (14) D.G. Yuengling	0.9	0.1	569.6
9. (30) Sierra Nevada	0.5	0.03	1509.6
10. Minnesota	0.4	[No Data]	

** The company's 1990 rank is in parentheses.* *** The percentage change is from 1990 to 2000.*

The New Belgium Brewing Company is the second largest in Colorado after Coors, with turn-of-the-century annual production of more than a quarter-million barrels. New Belgium is so named because company founder Jeff Lebesch is an aficionado of Belgian abbey-style ales and used yeast that he acquired in Belgium to brew his first commercial beers. He and his wife, Kim Jordan, began the New Belgium Brewing Company in their Fort Collins home in 1991 and moved to their present state-of-the-art brewery in 1995. New Belgium Brewing

New Belgium's flagship product, Fat Tire Amber Ale, is named because company founder Jeff Lebesch was riding a mountain bike across Belgium when he came up with the idea of taking some Belgian yeast home to Fort Collins. New Belgium Brewing

Piel, Rainier, Schmidt's, Stag, and the former New York–area giants, Ballantine and Schaefer. Most of the brewing plants, from the Rainier facility in Seattle to the Stroh brewery in Winston-Salem, were closed or sold by August 1999.

Pabst also retained the biggest names in the Stroh portfolio: Stroh's and Schlitz. Ironically, the two onetime Milwaukee rivals for the mantle of largest brewer in America were now under the same roof, and the roof was nowhere near Milwaukee. The Pabst corporate office now resides in San Antonio.

One Heileman brand that Pabst did keep somewhat near its roots was Lone Star. The erstwhile "National Beer of Texas," which was bought by Olympia of Washington in 1976 and by Heileman of Wisconsin in 1983, would no longer be brewed at the massive Lone Star brewery on the south side of San Antonio, but at the Pearl Brewing facility on the north side of town, which had been owned by Pabst since 1988. Between June 1999 and December 2002, both Pearl and Lone Star, the former cross-town rivals, were produced in the same facility.

A further chapter in the Pabst saga came at the end of 2002, when the onetime largest brewer in America ceased to brew beer entirely. From the beginning of 2003, Pabst became a "virtual brewer."

The big, stainless steel tanks at the Big Sky Brewing Company on Hickory Street in Missoula, Montana. Big Sky was the largest brewing company in Montana by the year 2000, and their flagship product, Moose Drool Brown Ale, was the best-selling draft beer made in the state. Big Sky Brewing

Firestone Walker uses a patented oak-barrel fermentation system based on the Burton Union system introduced in England around 1840. The 60-gallon, toasted-oak barrels impart distinctive flavor characteristics to the beer. Firestone Walker Brewing Company

Even after the opening of a much larger facility in Paso Robles, the original Firestone Walker taproom in Buellton, California, remains open. Featuring an antique bar pulled from London's Liverpool Street rail station, the taproom tempts patrons by offering taproom-only beers, such as India Pale Ale and an unfiltered version of Firestone Walker's signature Double Barrel Ale. Bill Yenne

The former Pearl Brewery on the north side of San Antonio was sold, and all of the Pabst brands were contract brewed by other companies elsewhere. In a twist that continued to link Pabst and Miller, Miller brewed the majority of those brands. Pearl and Lone Star, for example, were still produced in Texas, but at Miller's facility in Fort Worth.

Taking a long route around the block, Pabst began brewing its Heileman's Old Style at the old Heileman flagship brewery in LaCrosse, Wisconsin. Stroh had closed the plant after it acquired Heileman in 1996, and in 2000 the facility was acquired by a dozen local businessmen who renamed it the City Brewery. Historians will recall that this was the name given to the original brewery constructed on the site by John Gund and Gottlieb Heileman in 1858. The former Heileman brewery had initiated contract brewing, and had now wound up brewing one of the best-known former Heileman products!

With the exception of Leinenkugel, and arguably the Heileman/Pabst Texas brands, all the former regional icons that have been taken over by megabreweries have clearly lost identification with their roots. On the other hand, certain regional brands that have remained independent were revitalized at the turn of the century.

Adam Firestone (left) and David Walker started the Firestone Walker Brewing Company in 1995. Today, their beers are available on the California coast from San Diego to Santa Cruz. Firestone Walker Brewing Company

The most historically significant of these revitalized regionals is actually the oldest brewery in the United States. Dating back to 1829, the D.G. Yuengling Brewing Company of Pottsville, Pennsylvania, was one of a handful of American breweries to survive both the Civil War and Prohibition. It was one of an even smaller handful of family-owned regionals to survive the wave of consolidation that swept through the United States brewing industry after World War II. In 1985, as the Microbrewery Revolution was just beginning to sweep the country, Richard L. "Dick" Yuengling bought the family "microbrewery" from his father. He had big plans. In 1992, the brewery began the largest expansion in its 165-year history, and by 1997 the Pottsville brewery was producing over 500,000 barrels annually and exceeding capacity. To meet the demand, Yuengling acquired the former Stroh brewery in Tampa, Florida, in 1999, and constructed a new million-barrel brewery at St. Clair, a few miles northeast of Pottsville, which opened in 2001.

Brewmaster John Hybner at the Spoetzl Brewery in Shiner, Texas. The largest brewery in Texas not owned by a large out-of-state brewing company, Spoetzl was in the top ten nationally by the turn of the twenty-first century. Spoetzl Brewery

Above: *A chemist at work in the Spoetzl laboratory in Shiner, Texas. The big copper kettles of the brewhouse can be seen through the glass in the background.* Spoetzl Brewery

The 60-percent-plus sales increases posted by Latrobe and Pabst during the no-growth 1990s are good numbers, but the Yuengling ledger is even healthier: The Pottsville company posted an increase of 569.6 percent for the decade.

Yuengling's success was a corollary to the success of the Microbrewery Revolution. Dick Yuengling was able to capitalize on many of the same features that consumers found attractive with microbrews—a quality product from a small, family-run brewery, and a strong local following. It was pointed out in *Modern Brewery Age* magazine that "Pennsylvanians are the most loyal beer consumers in the country, and they have embraced Yuengling as their own." As the industry publication pointed out, Yuengling Brewing "worked on building extraordinary depth in its home state."

Another venerable family-owned regional brewery that made news at the turn of the century was August Schell Brewing in New Ulm, Minnesota. August Schell has a history similar to that of Yuengling, although it is a considerably newer company. Schell was not started until 1860, the same year that Abraham Lincoln was campaigning for his first term in the White House. When Schell opened its doors, Yuengling had been brewing for more than a quarter of a century. Nevertheless, both companies survived the Civil War, Prohibition, and the consolidation as independents with a strong local following. Schell was also a successful contract brewer, producing more than twenty brands in addition to its own.

By the turn of the century, August Schell was the number 34 brewery in the United States, with an annual output of 27,700 barrels. In 2002, this little fish swallowed a bigger fish, the troubled Minnesota Brewing Company of St. Paul—makers of the legendary Grain Belt brand—which officially ceased operations at the former Schmidt Brewery in June 2002. In 2000, Minnesota Brewing had been listed as the tenth-largest American brewer, with annual production of 371,000 barrels. In 2001, it had slipped to seventeenth place and just 90,000 barrels.

Ted Marti, president of the August Schell saw an opportunity to tap into Minnesota Brewing's distribution network, as well as to preserve the nostalgic Grain Belt name. A Twin Cities favorite since the time of Prohibition, Grain Belt was a longtime part of the Heileman portfolio of regional brand names before passing to Minnesota Brewing in 1991.

As the story of American brewing at the turn of the century continues to unfold, we have seen the implosion of the second-tier megabrewers. Anheuser-Busch and Coors remain as before, but the shuffle involving Miller, Stroh, Heileman, and Pabst has left only two standing and only Miller still

MARKET SHARE OF THE TOP TEN U.S. BREWING COMPANIES

Company	2000 Annual Output (Millions of Barrels)	PerPercent of U.S. Total
1. Anheuser-Busch	98.3	53.42
2. Miller	41.6	22.60
3. Coors	23.0	12.50
4. Pabst	10.5	5.70
5. Genesee	1.4	0.07
6. Boston Beer	1.2	0.06
7. Latrobe	1.2	0.06
8. D.G. Yuengling	0.9	0.05
9. Sierra Nevada	0.5	0.03
10. Minnesota	0.4	0.02

U.S. Output for 2000: 184 million barrels.

A worker at the Blitz-Weinhard Brewery in Portland, Oregon, pauses thoughtfully with a new stainless steel brew kettle gleaming in the background. His T-shirt carries the logo of Henry Weinhard's Private Reserve. As the company's premium product, it enjoyed great popularity in the 1980s after Heileman bought Blitz-Weinhard. Bill Yenne

Left: *The big stainless steel brew kettle at Blitz-Weinhard in Portland, Oregon. This kettle would brew for the last time in August 1999. Three years after Heileman sold the Blitz-Weinhard to Stroh, the brewery produced its last batch of beer and was closed forever.* Bill Yenne

brewing. The tale of the regional success stories, including Yuengling and Schell, can generally be attributed to the fact that people have developed a taste for thoughtfully brewed beers. This leads us to continue the story of the Microbrewery Revolution, which was born in the 1980s and which matured throughout the 1990s.

Now no longer a "revolution," microbreweries and craft breweries are a full-fledged market segment. If Yuengling's 569 percent growth during the 1990s looks good, consider the success enjoyed by craft brewers during the decade. Jim Koch's Boston Beer Company was up 1,008 percent, while Ken Grossman's Sierra Nevada Brewing Company leapt from thirtieth place to ninth among all American brewing companies with an increase of *more than* 1,500 percent for the decade.

Excluding the top five megabrewers, it would probably be safe to say that a growing three-quarters of the volume of beer sold in the United States at the turn of the century was brewed by brewing companies that did not exist before 1980.

Since the mid-1990s, even Anheuser-Busch has taken the notion of brewing quality, flavorful beers seriously. In 1994, the makers of Budweiser introduced the short-lived Elk Mountain Amber Ale and Elk Mountain Red Lager. The following year, Anheuser-Busch introduced several regional products designed to compete directly with craft beers that enjoyed strong local followings. In Texas, Anheuser-Busch's Ziegenbock competed with Shiner Bock from Spoetzl Brewing, while in the Northwest, Michelob HefeWeizen went head to head with the popular *hefewiezens* produced by Widmer and Pyramid. In 1996, Anheuser-Busch introduced Pacific Ridge Pale Ale, described as "an all-malt pale ale with a full-bodied taste and pronounced hop aroma." Initially available only in northern California, it would later be available elsewhere throughout the West.

The craft brewing industry would enjoy steady growth of 40 to 50 percent through most of the 1990s, until the recession of 1997 and 1998, when an industry shakeout led to a large number of well-publicized closings of marginal microbreweries. In Darwinian fashion, the stronger craft brewers weathered the storm and grew stronger, while the weak closed their doors. Those who had characterized the Microbrewery Revolution as a fad a decade earlier were quick to proclaim the end of microbreweries. However, like the much-heralded obituaries of Mark Twain and Rock & Roll, these epitaphs were more than premature. By 2001, new openings of microbreweries and brewpubs exceeded closings.

By the turn of the century, some of the most recognized names in the California wine industry were also getting into craft brewing. In 1995, Adam Firestone, the beer-loving son of Brooks Firestone, founder of the Firestone Vineyard—and the great grandson of tiremaker Harvey Firestone—decided to become a commercial brewer. As stated in *The Wine Spectator* in September 1996, "Faced with a shortage of grapes, one California vintner tried the next best thing. He made beer. Adam Firestone thought of the unique solution after the crop for the 1995 vintage in California's South Central coast was 50 to 80 percent smaller than expected."

Working with brother-in-law David Walker, Firestone began brewing an ale fermented in oak barrels. After an initial failure with used wine barrels, the partners scored a success with new oak. The Firestone Walker Brewing Company began operations in 1996, with a brewery and taproom near Buellton in northern Santa Barbara County. In 2002, the company moved to a new facility a few miles north at Paso Robles in San Luis Obispo County.

As the craft brewers are swift to note, it is not about quantity but quality. Gary Fish of Deschutes Brewery—twenty-first-ranked nationally—said, "This industry has more credibility now ... It has grown, and the quality of the beer has improved. Failures are just business, not a fad gone awry. We think there are very good times to come for this segment of the industry."

According to Institute of Brewing Studies statistics released in 2002, there were 1,458 craft breweries operating in the United States, up from the roughly 500 that had existed in the mid-1990s. This

Mass Bay Brewing Company head brewer Tod Mott bungs a well-worn half-keg of Harpoon Ale. In the background, Brian Donovan fills the next one. Mass Bay Brewing Company

brought the total number of breweries back to level that had not been seen since around 1910. Of the 2002 total, 999 were brewpubs, most producing fewer than a thousand barrels annually. Of the remainder, nearly fifty were "regional specialty" brewers, a new definition for those craft brewers that have grown beyond the 15,000-barrel annual production that is the definition of a "microbrewery."

At the turn of the century, companies such as Sierra Nevada, as well as New Belgium in Colorado and Deschutes in Oregon, enjoyed double-digit growth and a rapidly increasing regional market share. These, and a sizable number of other craft breweries, had moved past the 15,000-barrel level, and about half had production in excess of 30,000 barrels.

Three companies in Portland, Oregon, had moved into the category of "former microbreweries"—Portland Brewing, BridgePort Brewing, and Widmer Brothers all exceeded the 30,000-barrel level. Elsewhere in the Pacific Northwest, the Redhook Ale Brewery in Seattle; Full Sail Brewing in Hood River, Oregon; Pyramid Brewing in Kalama, Washington; Rogue in Newport, Oregon; and Alaskan Brewing of Juneau, Alaska, were no longer microbreweries. In California, Sierra Nevada and Anchor Brewing made the cut, as did Mendocino Brewing in Hopland, Lagunitas Brewing in Petaluma, and Anderson Valley Brewing in Boonville.

In addition to New Belgium, as of 2002 the Mountain West was home to three ex-micros: Odell Brewing in Fort Collins and Rockies Brewing in Boulder (founded in 1984 as Boulder Brewing), as well as Big Sky Brewing in Missoula, Montana, makers of the legendary Moose Drool Ale.

Certainly the craft brewing market was not solely a western phenomenon. In the Midwest and South, Boulevard Brewing in Kansas City; Summit Brewing in St. Paul; Goose Island Brewing in Chicago; Abita Brewing in Louisiana; Kalamazoo

NAMES AND LOCATIONS OF THE LEADING U.S. BREWING COMPANIES AT THE TURN OF THE TWENTY-FIRST CENTURY

Note: *Of the top four, Anheuser-Busch and Miller operate multiple breweries across the U.S., Coors operates two, and Pabst operates none, contracting out 100 percent of its production. The locations given for these multisite operators and for the brewpub chains (*****) are those of their corporate headquarters.*

Company	Location	2000 production in barrels
1. Anheuser-Busch	St. Louis, MO	98,300,000
2. Miller Brewing	Milwaukee, WI	41,229,000 ***
3. Adolph Coors	Golden, CO	22,994,000
4. Pabst Brewing	San Antonio, TX	10,500,000 *
5. Genesee Brewing	Rochester, NY	1,350,000 **
6. Boston Beer Company	Boston, MA	1,241,000 **
7. Latrobe Brewing	Latrobe, PA	1,150,000
8. D.G. Yuengling	Pottsville, PA	920,000
9. Sierra Nevada	Chico, CA	498,986
10. Minnesota Brewing	St. Paul, MN	371,000 ****
11. Leinenkugel Brewing	Chippewa Falls, WI	331,000
12. Matt Brewing	Utica, NY	276,000
13. Pittsburgh	Pittsburgh, PA	275,000
14. Spoetzl Brewery	Shiner, TX	261,727
15. Redhook Ale Brewery	Seattle, WA	212,600
16. New Belgium Brewing	Fort Collins, CO	164,800
17. Pete's Brewing	Palo Alto, CA	151,975 *
18. Widmer Brothers	Portland, OR	127,000
19 Pyramid Breweries	Kalama, WA	109,945
20. Anchor Brewing	San Francisco, CA	97,000
21. Deschutes Brewing	Bend, OR	95,272
22. Alaskan Brewing	Juneau, AK	83,354
23. Portland Brewing	Portland, OR	68,209
24. Full Sail Brewing	Hood River, OR	64,884
25. Gordon Biersch	San Jose, CA	60,237 *****
26. Joseph Huber Brewing	Monroe, WI	60,000
27. Mass Bay Brewing	Boston, MA	53,100
28. Stevens Point	Stevens Point, WI	50,000
29. Mendocino Brewing	Hopland, CA	49,255
30. Dixie Brewing	New Orleans, LA	46,000
31. Jones Brewing	Smithton, PA	43,380
32. Goose Island	Chicago, IL	43,000 +
33. Summit Brewing	St. Paul, MN	42,904
34. Hudepohl-Schoenling	Cincinnati, OH	40,676
35. Boulevard Brewing	Kansas City, MO	39,339
36. Straub Brewing	St. Mary"s, PA	36,041

continued on page 147

Company	Location	2000 production in barrels
37. Abita Brewing	Abita Springs, LA	34,500
38. Brooklyn Brewery	Brooklyn, NY	31,906
39. Shipyard Brewery	Portland, ME	30,985
40. BridgePort Brewing	Portland, OR	30,720
41. Frederick Brewing	Frederick, MD	29,772+
42. August Schell	New Ulm, MN	27,700 ****
43. Hops Restaurants	Tampa, FL	26,723 + ****
44. Old Dominion Brewing	Ashburn, VA	26,640
45. Magic Hat Brewing	Burlington, VT	26,100
46. City Brewery	LaCrosse, WI	25,550
47. Kalamazoo Brewing	Kalamazoo, MI	24,657
48. Otter Creek Brewing	Middlebury, VT	24,492
49. Pennsylvania Brewing	Pittsburgh, PA	22,000
50. Odell Brewing	Fort Collins, CO	20,592
51. McMenamin's	Portland, OR	19,588 *****
52. Rogue Ales	Newport, R	19,300 +
53. Utah Brewers	Salt Lake City, UT	18,011
54. Great Lakes Brewing	Cleveland, OH	17,927
55. Rockies Brewing	Boulder, CO	17,852
56. Anderson Valley	Boonville, CA	17,731
57. Big Sky Brewing	Missoula, MT	17,200 +
58. Golden Pacific	Emeryville, CA	16,129
59. D.L. Geary Brewing	Portland, ME	15,822
60. Celis Brewery	Austin, TX	15,070
61. Lagunitas Brewing	Lagunitas, CA	14,809
62. North Coast Brewing	Fort Bragg, CA	14,639
63. Sprecher Brewing	Milwaukee, WI	14,118
64. Uinta Brewing	Salt Lake City, UT	13,749
65. Capital Brewery	Middleton, WI	13,369
66. Hale's Ales	Seattle, WA	13,220

** Indicates a "contract" brewer whose beer is produced at another brewery*
*** Indicates a brewery whose totals include some contract-brewed beer*
**** Leinenkugel is a wholly owned subsidiary of Miller Brewing, but the data is shown separately because Leinenkugel is treated as a separate operating unit*
***** Minnesota Brewing closed its doors in 2002. Its flagship brand, Grain Belt, was acquired by August Schell*
****** Gordon Biersch, McMenamin's, and Hops are chains of brewpubs and brewery restaurants*
+ 2002 data is given because 2000 data is unavailable

Symbolic of the brewing renaissance in the South is the Southend chain of brewery restaurants. The original Southend Brewery started up in Charlotte, North Carolina, in April 1995; this brewery in Charleston, South Carolina, opened in June 1996 in a building that dates from 1880. Other Southend brewpubs were added in Raleigh and Jacksonville during 1999, and a site in Lake Norman, North Carolina, opened in 2000. Bill Yenne

Brewing in Michigan; and Great Lakes Brewing in Duluth, Minnesota, joined the ranks of "regional specialty" brewers.

In the East, Boston's Mass Bay; Frederick Brewing in Maryland, the Shipyard Brewery in Portland, Maine; and *two* Vermont companies—Magic Hat and Otter Creek—all moved into the category of regional brewing companies that were formerly microbreweries. In 2000, Mass Bay became even larger through the acquisition of Catamount, Vermont's original microbrewery. Founded in the railroad town of White River Junction in 1987, Catamount had constructed a large new brewing facility in Windsor, Vermont. Mass Bay would brew

The Gordon Biersch Brewery Restaurant in the Burbank Village district of the city of Burbank, north of Los Angeles. About one-third of the two dozen Gordon Biersch breweries (opened in the decade since Dan Gordon and Dean Biersch opened their first brewery in Palo Alto in 1988) are located in California. Dana Kemberling, Gordon Biersch

both the former Catamount products, as well as its own Harpoon product line, at Windsor.

By the turn of the century, several contract brewers had outputs that exceeded the 31,000-gallon limit. There were Jim Koch's Boston Beer Company, Brooklyn Brewery of New York, and California-based Pete's, makers of the well-known "Pete's Wicked" family of beers.

Brewpubs, because their marketing area is usually limited to their own premises and a small takeout business, are typically not large enough to exceed the 15,000-barrel number. However, at the turn of the century, three *chains* of brewpubs had achieved that level: the Tampa-based Hops Restaurant/Brewery chain, McMenamin's western Oregon brewpub

Right: *A view of the Miller-owned "Olympia" Brewery at Tumwater, Washington as seen from Capital Way. Hamm's acquired the brewery in 1983 and was swallowed by Pabst parent S&P two years later. After Miller took control in 1999, it began brewing Olympia at the facility under contract to Pabst. The trucks, however, were still*

archipelago, and the San Jose–based Gordon Biersch brewery-restaurant chain, which also maintained a bottling operation.

Craft-brewed beer had arrived and was here to stay. Massive advertising budgets and thorough market penetration kept the megabrewers at the top of the industry, but hundreds of thousands of beer lovers, reared on quality craft-brewed beers for two decades or more, may never go back to mass-market lagers. The onetime "fad" had redefined what Americans thought of as beer.

One of the most important effects of the aftermath of the Microbrewery Revolution has been on the way consumers have come to once again identify with local and regional products. By the turn of the twenty-first century, as the microbreweries morphed into regional specialty brewers, a phenomenon not seen in a generation returned to most of the country. In New England, they went for Harpoon as their grandfathers had for Narragansett. In New York City, Brooklyn Lager earned a loyalty once bestowed upon Rheingold. In Montana, those who could barely remember Highlander or Great Falls Select in Grandma's fridge, embraced Moose Drool and Scapegoat. In California, the granddaughters of Acme or Lucky Lager devotees now proudly ordered Anderson Valley Boont Amber or Mendocino's Red Tail Ale.

As the efficiently managed specialty brewers have thrived and grown at a rate that has outstripped that of the megabrewers, it is clear that craft brewing and craft-brewed beers are now the leading edge of the industry as it proceeds into the twenty-first century.

The Gordon Biersch Brewery Restaurant in Honolulu is located adjacent to the famous Aloha Tower near the city's downtown area, rather than in the more tourist-oriented Waikiki district. For this reason, more than two thirds of the patrons are locals rather than tourists. Although beer is not indigenous to Hawaii, the food menu specifically features elements of traditional Hawaiian cuisine. Dana Kemberling, Gordon Biersch

GLOSSARY

Ale: A top-fermented beer that originated in England as early as the seventh century and which has been made with hops since about the sixteenth century. It is fermented at temperatures ranging between 55 and 70 degrees Fahrenheit (13 and 21 degrees Celsius), somewhat warmer than those used to ferment lager. It is the primary beer type in England and among North American microbreweries, but is extremely rare elsewhere. It is, however, a close cousin to the German *altbier*. Subtypes include pale ale (which is actually much more amber than pale lagers), brown ale, and India pale ale, a beer developed in the nineteenth century by English brewers for export to the Empire.

Altbier: The German equivalent of English or American ale, literally a beer made in the "old" way (pre–nineteenth century) with top-fermenting yeast. Indigenous to Dusseldorf, Germany, and surrounding environs, it was virtually unknown in the United States after Prohibition, but was reintroduced by several microbreweries in Oregon and California during the 1980s.

Barley Wine: In Britain, ales with alcohol contents approaching that of wine (sometimes surpassing 10 percent by volume) are called barley wines.

Barrel: A container for beer, at one time made of reinforced oak, now made of stainless steel or aluminum. Also a unit of measurement for beer which equals 31 gallons, or 1.2 hectoliters.

Beer: A general term for *all* fermented malt beverages flavored with hops. The term embraces ale, lager, porter, stout, and all other types discussed herein. Ingredients include malted cereal grains, especially (but not limited to) barley, hops, yeast, and water, although early English beers were unhopped.

Subtypes are classified by whether they are made with top-fermenting yeast (ale, porter, stout, and wheat beer) or bottom-fermenting yeast (lager, bock beer, malt liquor). Generally, top-fermented beers are darker, ranging from a translucent copper to opaque black, while bottom-fermented beers range from amber to pale yellow. Because of their respective heritages, top-fermented beers are usually drunk at room temperature, while bottom-fermented beers are served cold.

Bier: The German, Dutch, and Flemish word for beer.

Bière: The French word for beer.

Birra: The Italian word for beer.

Bitter: A full-bodied, highly hopped ale (hence the name) that is extremely popular in England but much less so elsewhere. Bitter (or bitter ale) is similar in color to other ales, but lacks carbonation and has a slightly higher alcohol content. Also, a noun used in England to identify highly hopped ale. Originally, it was probably short for bitter ale. The less-used antonym is "mild," also a noun, which implies a lightly hopped English ale.

Bock Beer: A bottom-fermented beer that is darker than lager and which has a relatively higher alcohol content, usually in the 6 percent range. Bock originated in Germany and most German brewers still brew it as a special supplement to their principal product lines.

A seasonal beer, bock is traditionally associated with spring festivals. Prior to World War II, many American brewers produced a bock beer each spring, but the advent of national marketing after the war largely eliminated seasonal beers. In the 1980s, several breweries began to reintroduce bock beer. The male goat (*bock* in German) is the traditional symbol of bock beer. Subtypes include *doppelbock*, a bock especially high in alcohol, and *maibock*, a bock marketed in conjunction with May festivals.

Brasserie: The French word for brewery. Also, a small café.

Bräuerei: The German word for brewery.

Brewing: Generically, the entire beer-making process, but technically only that part of the process during which the wort is cooked in a brew kettle, during which time the hops are added. Following the brewing, beer is fermented.

Brewpub: A pub or tavern that brews its own beer on the premises. Brewpubs existed in Boston in 1639 and were common through the nineteenth century. With the enactment of the Eighteenth Amendment in 1920, they disappeared completely for six decades. Until the early 1980s, as a holdover from Prohibition laws, it was illegal in most states and Canadian provinces to both brew beer and sell it directly on the same site. Subsequent changes in local laws have rescinded these outdated restrictions and have made it possible for brewpubs to become more widespread.

A brewpub differs from a *microbrewery* in that its primary market is under its own roof. Some brewpubs bottle their beers for sale to patrons and for wholesale to retailers, while some microbreweries also operate brewpubs, so the distinction between the two can be somewhat blurred. Both, however, share a commitment to their own unique beers, and most brewpublicans entered their trade out of a love for brewing and an interest in distinctive beer styles.

Brouwerij: The Dutch and Flemish word for brewery.

Cerveceria: The Spanish word for brewery.

Cerveja: The Portuguese word for beer.

Cerveza: The Spanish word for beer.

Cream Ale: A blend of ale and lager invented in the early twentieth century by American brewers.

Diat: A German word for lager low in carbohydrates originally developed for diabetics. It is *not* a "diet" or low-calorie beer.

Doppelbock: A German word meaning literally "double bock". Although it is not nearly twice as strong as *bock*, it is typically the highest alcohol (over seven percent by volume) beer style brewed in Germany but lower in alcohol than English *barley wine*. In naming practice, doppelbocks are given names ending in "ator," such as Celebrator, Salvator, and Optimator.

Draft (Draught): A term that describes beer that is drawn from a keg rather than packaged in bottles or cans. Designed for immediate use, draft beer is not pasteurized and hence must be kept cold to prevent the loss of its fresh taste. Draft beer is generally better than packaged beer when fresh but not so as it ages. Some brewers sell unpasteurized draft-style beers in cans and bottles, which must be shipped in refrigerated containers.

Dry Beer: A pale lager in which all the fermentable sugars from the original malt have been converted to alcohol. In order to conclude the process with a beer of acceptable alcohol content (roughly 3.2 percent by weight), a brewer must start with less malt. Hence, dry beer has a low original gravity and will have very little flavor unless it is more heavily hopped than typical beers. The process is similar to that used by brewers to produce light beer, and the results are very similar. In fact, most American mass-market lagers, including light and dry beers, are very similar in taste. Beers in which all fermentable sugars are fermented were developed in Germany and Switzerland in the 1970s as *diat* beer designed for diabetics.

Dunkel (Dunkles): A German adjective used to describe a dark lager, usually in the sweeter Munich style.

Eisbock: A German term that originated in Dortmund and which is applied to especially flavorful and powerful light-colored lagers.

ESB (Extra Special Bitter): A term that originated in England for describing a brewer's best highly hopped bitter ale.

Export: This style evolved when the brewers in Dortmund, Germany, began transporting beer to other markets across the continent. In order to withstand the rigors of travel, they produced a beer that was well hopped and slightly higher in alcohol. As such, the Dortmund lager as a style is known as "export". Dortmund lagers are traditionally full-bodied but not quite as sweet as the beers of Munich and not as dry as true pilsners. Beers identified as such are not necessarily brewed specifically to be exported, although they often are.

Fermentation: The process by which yeast turns the sugars present in malted grains into alcohol and carbon dioxide. Chemically, the process is written as:

$$C_6H_{12}O_6 \rightarrow 2\,C_2H_5OH + 2\,CO_2$$

(glucose)(alcohol)(carbon dioxide)

Gueuze: Blended Belgian *lambic* beers not containing fruits.

Helles: A German adjective meaning "bright" that is commonly used in that country to describe lager that is pale in color.

Hops: The dried blossom of the female hop plant which is a climbing herb (*Humulus lupulus*) native to temperate regions of the Northern Hemisphere and cultivated in Europe, the United Kingdom, and the United States. Belonging to the mulberry family, the hop's leaves and flowers are characterized by a bitter taste and aroma. It has been used since the ninth century as the principal flavoring and seasoning agent in brewing, although it had been prized before that for its medicinal properties. In addition to its aromatic resins, the hop also contains tannin which helps to clarify beer.

Different strains of hops have different properties and much of the brewmaster's art is in knowing how to use these properties. For example, one strain may be particularly bitter to the taste without being very aromatic, while another strain might be just the opposite. The brewmaster will blend the two in various combinations just as a chef experiments with various seasonings before settling on just the right combination for a particular recipe. Hops also serve as a natural preservative.

Ice Beer: Developed and patented by Labatt in Canada, ice beer is a pale lager that is quickly chilled to sub-freezing temperatures after brewing but before final fermentation. The result is the formation of ice crystals in the beer, which are removed to produce a beer with roughly twice the alcohol content of typical mass-market lagers.

IPA (India Pale Ale): A type of highly hopped but light-colored ale developed in England in the late eighteenth century designed specifically to not deteriorate in quality during the long voyage to India.

Keller: A German-style of packaged, unfiltered lager that emulates *vom fass* (draft) beer.

Krausening (Kraeusening): The process of instigating a secondary fermentation to produce additional carbon dioxide in a beer. Some brewers first ferment their beer in open containers where alcohol is produced and retained, but the carbon dioxide escapes. The second fermentation, or krausening, takes place in closed containers after a first fermentation (whether that first fermentation took place in open or closed containers) to produce natural carbonation or sparkle.

Kriek: A Belgian *lambic* flavored with cherries. Probably the most popular of the fruit lambics.

Lager: This beer style accounts for well over 90 percent of the beer brewed and marketed in the world outside England. Specifically, it is a clear, pale beer fermented with bottom- fermenting yeast at nearly freezing temperatures. The fermentation period is also longer than that for ale and hence the name, which is German for "to store."

Lager had its origins in the heart of central Europe in an area that the author likes to call the Golden Triangle, so named because of the golden color of lager itself and because of the success that brewers had with this product when it was first developed for widespread commercial sale in the early to middle nineteenth century. The corners of the triangle are Munich, Prague, and Vienna, the capitals, respectively, of Bavaria (a state of the German Federal Republic), Bohemia (Czech Republic), and Austria.

Lambic: A style of beer fermented with special strains of wild yeast indigenous only to Belgium's Senne Valley. One of the world's most unique native beer styles.

Lauter Tun: The vessel used in brewing between the *mash tun* and the brew kettle. Here, the barley husks are separated from the clear liquid *wort*. The barley husks help provide a natural filter bed through which the wort is strained.

Lautering: The process of straining *wort* in a *lauter tun* before it is cooked in the brew kettle.

Light Beer: Introduced in the mid-1970s by nearly every major brewer in the United States and Canada, light beers are by definition reduced-calorie lagers or ales. They also have a slightly lower alcohol content than comparable lagers or ales.

Maibock: A *bock* beer brewed for release in May.

Malt Liquor: A bottom-fermented beer, it has a malty taste more closely related to top-fermented ale than to bottom-fermented lager. Malt liquor also has a much higher alcohol content (5.6 to 6.5 percent) than lager.

Also, a term imposed by the American government to identify beer with an alcohol content above 5 percent. It is not actually a true beer type, as the term may be used to describe ales or lagers. Some larger American brewers produce very pale, high-alcohol lagers and call them malt liquors.

Malting: The process by which barley kernels are moistened and germinated, producing a "green malt" that is then dried. This renders the starches in the kernel soluble. If pale beers are to be produced, the malt is simply dried. If dark beers are to be produced, the malt is roasted until it is dark brown. The malt is then subjected to *mashing*.

Märzen: Originally this German term was used to describe a reddish lager brewed in March and then set aside for summer. The style is now brewed for autumn consumption, particularly in connection with Oktoberfest.

Mash: The substance produced by mashing.

Mash Tun: Vessel in which barley is mashed.

Mashing: The process by which barley malt is mixed with water and cooked to turn soluble starch into fermentable sugar. Other cereal grains, such as corn and rice, may also be added (rice contributes to a paler beer). After mashing in a *mash tun*, the mash is filtered through a *lauter tun*, whereupon it becomes known as *wort*.

Microbrewery: A microbrewery was originally considered to be a brewery with a capacity of less than 3,000 barrels per year, but by the end of the 1980s this threshold increased to 15,000 barrels, as the demand for microbrewed beer doubled and then *tripled*.

Near Beer: Nonalcoholic beer that originated during the Prohibition era in the United States and which is still in production.

Pasteurization: Though this term has come to mean the heating of a substance to kill harmful bacteria, the process was originally proposed by Louis Pasteur as a means of killing yeast to end fermentation and hence end the creation of alcohol and carbon dioxide (carbonation). Nonpasteurized beers are no less sanitary than pasteurized beers.

Pils: A German term for pale, pilsen-style lagers.

Pilsener or Pilsner: A pale, bottom-fermented lager beer originally associated with the city of Pilsen, Bohemia (Czech Republic), where it was first brewed in the early nineteenth century. The term is often used interchangeably with the term *lager*, although pilsners are technically the palest of lagers.

Pilsners are also the most widely known and widely imitated lager type. The Plzensky Prazdroj brewery in Pilsen brews Pilsner Urquell ("Pilsner from the original source"), which is considered the definitive pilsner, although the term has become generic.

Porter: A dark, sweet beer brewed with top-fermenting (ale-type) yeast that was developed in London in the late eighteenth century and revived by American microbrewers in the late twentieth century. It derives its name from the London's porters, who took an immediate fancy to it. Similar to but sweeter than stout, it is a dark beer of moderate strength (5 to 7 percent alcohol by volume), made with roasted, unmalted barley.

Prohibition: The process by which a government prohibits its citizens from buying or possessing alcoholic beverages. Specifically, *the* Prohibition refers to the period between the effective date of the Eighteenth Amendment to the U.S. Constitution (January 16, 1920) and its repeal by the Twenty-first Amendment. Repeal took effect on December 5, 1933, although it passed Congress in February and the sale of beer was permitted after April 7, 1933.

Rauchbier: A lager that derives a wonderfully flavor from malted grain that has been roasted over a very smoky beechwood fire. Indigenous to the Bamberg area in southern Germany, *rauchbier* means literally "smoked beer." Smoked beer, which is rare outside of Germany, is generally served with meals including smoked or barbecued meats, rye breads, and certain sharp cheeses.

Reinheitsgebot: A German purity law enacted in 1516 that permits only malted barley, hops, yeast, and water to be used in the brewing of beer sold in Germany. Though it has no jurisdiction outside Germany, many North American brewers follow it, and some use the fact that they meet its guidelines as part of their advertising. Since Germany's admission to the European community, the Reinheitsgebot has not been legally binding since 1987, but German brewers still proudly follow it.

Sake: A fermented beverage that is a cousin to the family of fermented beverages we call beer. Sake originated in Japan where it is an important national drink. Several sake breweries have existed in both California and Hawaii over the years, but the only remaining American commercial sake brewery is in Hawaii. Sake is brewed from unmalted rice and is not hopped. The resulting substance is clear and has a 14 to 16 percent alcohol content. In contrast to beer, which is drunk either chilled or at room temperature, sake is warmed before drinking.

Steam Beer: A term that originated in San Francisco during the Gold Rush era to describe beer that was produced with bottomfermenting yeast but fermented at 60 to 70 degrees Fahrenheit (15 to 21 degrees Celsius), rather than the temperatures required for true lager fermentation. Fermentation was allowed to continue in the kegs and the escaping carbon dioxide that resulted from their tapping is the possible source of the term "steam" beer. In any event, the term is now a registered trademark of The Anchor Brewing Company of San Francisco, brewers of Anchor Steam Beer.

Stout: A dark, heavy, top-fermented beer popular in the British Isles, especially Ireland (where Guinness stout is more popular than Budweiser lager is in the United States). It is similar to porter, though less sweet. Its alcohol content ranges from 4 to 7 percent.

Stout is a dark, creamy beer produced with top-fermenting (ale type) yeast. Stout is the prominent beer type in Ireland and is widely available in England. Also brewed occasionally by microbreweries in the United States, it is not nearly so popular in continental Europe. Guinness, brewed in Dublin and London, is the definitive stout of the Irish type. It is also brewed under license in many places throughout the world. English brewers, such as Samuel Smith in Tadcaster, also produce oatmeal stout, in which oats are used along with barley malt.

Tesguino: A type of corn beer produced by the natives of Mexico and the American Southwest prior to their contact with Europeans.

Vom Fass: German phrase for "on tap."

Wheat Beer: Although beer, by definition, is derived from malted barley, other grains, such as rice and cornmeal, are often used in less-expensive, mass-market brands as a cheap source of starch, a practice is frowned upon by discriminating brewers and consumers. Exceptions are made in the case of oats in English oatmeal stout and with wheat in American wheat beer, German *weissbier,* and Flemish *witbier*. Both the German and Flemish terms are literally translated as meaning "white" beer, a reference to the light color of the beer and the fact that it usually has yeast particles in suspension. In Germany, *weissbiers* that are cloudy are identified with the prefix *hefe* (yeast) as *hefeweissbier*, or simply *hefeweiss*.

Weissbier: A German word literally meaning beer that is white (weiss), but actually implying a style of pale-colored, top- fermented beer made with about half wheat malt. It is typical of Berlin and northern Europe. Weissbier is also known as *weizenbier*, but should not be confused with *wiesenbier*, which is a festival beer that may or may not contain wheat malt.

Witbier/Bière Blanche: Flemish/French literally meaning white (wit/blanche) beer. It is brewed using over half wheat malt. A cousin to German *weissbier*, *witbier* is indigenous to the northern, Flemish-speaking areas of Belgium.

Wort: An oatmeal-like substance consisting of water and mashed barley in which soluble starch has been turned into fermentable sugar during the mashing process. The *wort* is cooked, or brewed, in the brew kettle for more than an hour and for as much as a day, during which time hops are added to season the *wort*. After brewing, the hopped *wort* is filtered and fermented to produce beer.

Yeast: The enzyme-producing, one-celled fungi of the genus *Saccharomyces* that is added to wort before the fermentation process for the purpose of turning fermentable sugar into alcohol and carbon dioxide.

INDEX

WIELANDS
WIELANDS
WIELANDS
WIELANDS
WIELANDS
WIELANDS
John Wieland's
Extra
Pale
John Wieland Brewery
SAN FRANCISCO U.S.A
BREWERY'S OWN BOTTLING
John Wieland's